Ghosts of Greater Los Angeles

Preston Dennett

Illustrations by Kesara

Schiffer Publishing Ltd

4880 Lower Valley Road, Atglen, Pennsylvania 19310

Dedication

To my father
who now journeys in the afterlife...

Published by Schiffer Publishing Ltd.
4880 Lower Valley Road
Atglen, PA 19310
Phone: (610) 593-1777; Fax: (610) 593-2002
E-mail: Info@schifferbooks.com

For the largest selection of fine reference books on this and related subjects, please visit our web site at: **www.schifferbooks.com**
We are always looking for people to write books on new and related subjects.
If you have an idea for a book please contact us at the above address.

This book may be purchased from the publisher.
Include $5.00 for shipping.
Please try your bookstore first.
You may write for a free catalog.

In Europe, Schiffer books are distributed by
Bushwood Books
6 Marksbury Ave.
Kew Gardens
Surrey TW9 4JF England
Phone: 44 (0) 20 8392 8585; Fax: 44 (0) 20 8392 9876
E-mail: info@bushwoodbooks.co.uk
Website: www.bushwoodbooks.co.uk

Other Schiffer Books by Preston Dennett:
Supernatural California, 0-7643-2401-2, $24.95
California Ghosts: True Accounts of Hauntings in the Golden State, 0-7643-1972-8, $14.95
UFOs Over California: A True History of Extraterrestrial Encounters in the Golden State, 0-7643-2149-8, $14.95
UFOs Over New York: A True History of Extraterrestrial Encounters in the Empire State, 978-0-7643-2974-6, $16.99

Other Schiffer Books on Related Subjects:
Ghosts of Orange County, 978-0-7643-3171-8, $14.99
Coastal Ghosts of Southern California, 978-0-7643-3150-3, $14.99
Ghosts of San Francisco, 978-0-7643-2765-0, $12.95

Library of Congress Control Number: 2010926109

Designed by Mark David Bowyer
Type set in A Charming Font Superexpanded / New Baskerville

ISBN: 978-0-7643-3503-7
Printed in the United States of America

Contents

Introduction

Do you believe in ghosts? Would you like to see one? It might be a lot easier than you think. Despite the fact that some people still remain skeptical, the truth is that ghost researchers have made considerable progress in proving the veracity of ghosts. They have not only gathered sufficient evidence to nearly prove that ghosts are real, but they have also discovered how many hauntings begin, how they evolve, and how they end. They know how ghosts manifest and why — and most importantly, ghost researchers have identified literally thousands of locations across the United States and throughout the world that are known to have ghostly activity.

Of course ghosts are real! Skeptics vastly underestimate the amount of evidence. There are literally tens of thousands of eyewitness reports stretching back thousands of years and appearing in virtually every culture on earth. More recently scientists and ghost hunters have been able to bring science and technology into the study of ghosts. As a result, we now have a vast array of evidence, including photographs and film of moving apparitions and/or objects moving by themselves, audio EVP (Electronic Voice Phenomena) recordings, EMF readings from electromagnetic detectors, and recorded temperature fluctuations correlated with ghostly activity.

While the circumstantial evidence for ghosts is overwhelming, their existence still has not been conclusively proven. At least, the evidence is tenuous enough that mainstream science continues to deny that ghosts are real. Because of that, the subject of ghosts falls into the catchall category labeled "the paranormal." Of course, there is no such thing as "paranormal." When something so-called "unexplainable" happens, it doesn't mean that the Laws of the

Universe have been violated. Instead, it is an indication that our knowledge of these laws is incomplete. Unexplainable is simply misunderstood.

Although ghosts are often considered unexplainable, it's pretty obvious to most people what they are: spirits of the deceased. However, most researchers believe that ghosts come in several different varieties.

Types of Ghosts

† First, there are spirits. *Spirits* are the souls of people (and animals) who have died. Spirits manifest for a variety of reasons. Some have experienced sudden, tragic deaths and are not aware that they have died. Some are attached to their homes or to loved ones and refuse to leave, or perhaps are just coming to visit. Some suffer from addictions that overcome them and force them to remain earthbound and attempt to satisfy their physical cravings. Others might be consumed with emotions, such as guilt, anger, or something else that is keeping them attached to the physical world. Many spirits have a purpose, manifesting for a particular reason such as saying goodbye, providing the location of missing documents or money, or giving a vital message concerning an important personal or business issue. Probably the majority of ghostly activity is of this first type — the spirit.

† Another popular theory to explain some ghost activity is known as the *poltergeist*, which is a German word meaning noisy ghost. Researchers have discovered that poltergeist activity often (but not always) occurs in the presence of a pubescent teenager and seems to be linked to their mental and emotional state. Poltergeist activity is typically intense, mischievous, and brief, though this is not always the case. In these cases, some researchers theorize that there is no actual ghost. Instead the activity is the result of uncontrolled psychokinesis or telekinesis. The repressed emotional/mental energy from the teenager (and

sometimes adults) explodes and manifests in the form of the uncontrolled movement of objects, electromagnetic disturbances, mysterious noises, and other paranormal events. Also, some researchers have theorized that poltergeist hauntings might be better explained as *uncontrolled mediumship*, which is a subject we will explore later in the book.

† A third theory is that some ghosts are actually non-human entities, or *demons*, consumed with a hatred for God and humanity and attempt to possess the unwary. The careless use of a Ouija Board® or the calling forth of spirits, some researchers say, can lead to demonic possession. This theory is among the most controversial and hotly debated, but yet the belief in demons remains widespread across the United States and throughout the world.

† A fourth theory that is gaining increasing popularity is known as a *residual haunting*. In these cases, the ghosts may seem real, but they are in reality just echoes of past events. This theory was adopted when researchers realized that in many cases, the ghosts did not seem to perceive the outside environment and instead just re-enacted the same event or events over and over again. The theory is that events involving extreme emotions or trauma are somehow recorded into the environment where they occurred. In these cases, the activity is predictable and repetitive. The spirit and the consciousness of the person is not really there and can therefore neither interact nor perceive living people. Instead, the activity is just an echo, replaying the same event again and again.

† Another theory is that some ghost activity can be explained as a kind of *time-slip*. Under this model, ghosts are, in fact, living people going about their daily lives as they lived them in the past, but are somehow being perceived by people living in the present. This theory is supported by the many cases of people who have seen ghostly people, ghostly trees and plants, ghostly structures, ghostly vehicles, and, in some rare cases, entire ghostly environments.

Growing in Popularity

Whatever the explanation for ghosts, they can no longer be denied. The countless books, television programs, and Internet websites on the subject is evidence of their popularity, and one of the most exciting things about ghost research today is that ghost hunters have been able to identify literally thousands of locations where ghosts appear. Research has become specialized to the point where the known haunted locations in each city across the United States have been pinpointed and recorded for posterity.

This book presents the story behind many of the known and unknown haunted locations in the Greater Los Angeles area of Southern California. New information and firsthand interviews with actual witnesses are provided at each location. Some of the hauntings are famous — the Hollywood Roosevelt Hotel is perhaps one of the most haunted hotels in Los Angeles. Others are less well known, such as Universal Studios or Forest Lawn Cemetery. Some have never been published before, including an area near Glendale where numerous children have encountered ghostly Native American children or the case of a major hospital in Van Nuys, where several nurses are reporting incredible experiences in a certain room. There are also other cases of haunted houses and apartment buildings and much more. Both public and private hauntings are equally represented. In all of these cases, you will read incredible accounts of people who have come face-to-face with the unknown all across Southern California.

Why Los Angeles?

Los Angeles, the City of Angels, could appropriately be called the city of spirits. Established in 1850, the city today has literally dozens of active public hauntings and countless residential hauntings taking place within a radius of a few hundred miles. While the majority of hauntings probably take place at private residences, there are just as many public locations — hotels, theaters, businesses, office buildings, missions, museums, parks, graveyards, roadways — that also experience activity. Los Angeles and the surrounding areas, it turns out, are extremely haunted.

Why is this area so haunted? The simple answer is because, like any major megalopolis, there are a lot of people. It makes sense that the level of ghostly activity would correspond with the size of the population when you consider that ghosts are, in fact, people.

The ghosts of Greater Los Angeles do have their own unique flavor and colorful history. Some of the cases involve the spirits of Native Americans who still haunt the locations where they once lived many years ago. Some involve long-dead celebrities who remain, clinging to the locations where they led their glamourous lives of fame and fortune. Some involve accounts of sad and lonely child ghosts. All, however, involve people who suddenly find themselves in the unfortunate position of having become a ghost.

Although many people regard spirits and ghostly activity with fear and confusion, the evidence shows that, for the most part, they are just like us! In most cases ghosts are just people and need not be feared. Instead of being afraid, some people, including many ghost researchers, actively seek out ghosts and even hope to catch a glimpse of an apparition or to see an object move by itself.

As it turns out, if you want to see a ghost, Southern California is an excellent place to start. This area is literally teeming with ghostly activity. This book provides all the tools you need to see your own ghost. Complete directions are provided to the many locations. So get your flashlight and camera and get ready to travel across the southland as we visit the many haunted locations in Greater Los Angeles.

"Looking into the mirror, she was shocked to see an image of an attractive blond woman... At first she didn't recognize the face. However, she soon learned that the mirror had, in fact, belonged to Marilyn Monroe."

Chapter One

Hollywood Roosevelt Hotel Revisited

7000 Hollywood Boulevard
Los Angeles, California
323-466-7000

As any ghost researcher will tell you, one of the most common types of haunted locations are hotels. The question is why?

Some researchers believe that the reason is because hotels are visited by a wide variety of people who conduct a wide variety of activities there. Any single hotel room may be visited by hundreds of people in one year alone. When you consider the fact that many of the hotels in Los Angeles are decades old, it is little wonder that they aren't all haunted.

Probably the most famous and unique of all of LA's haunted hotels is the Hollywood Roosevelt. Built in 1921 and named after President Theodore Roosevelt, the five-star luxury hotel represented the very best accommodations that Hollywood had to offer at that time. It towers twelve stories and contains 320 rooms, thirty-eight suites, and sixty-five poolside cabana rooms.

The building was designed to cater to the rich and famous and, from its opening day, it attracted a long list of old-time celebrities including such luminaries as Douglas Fairbanks, Greta Garbo, Clark Gable, Charlie Chaplin, Will Rogers, Mary Pickford, Harold Lloyd, Gloria Swanson, Clifton Webb, Carole Lombard, and Montgomery Clift...to name a few!

Some of the most famous photographs of Marilyn Monroe were taken in the hotel pool. Shirley Temple took some of her first dance lessons on the hotel staircase. During the Prohibition era, Errol Flynn used the hotel's barber room to make batches of gin. The hotel was the location of the first Academy Awards and became *The Place To Be* for anybody who wanted to rub elbows with Hollywood royalty.

For more than sixty years, the hotel worked in relative peace and prosperity. Though renovated, minimally, a few times, by the mid-1980s it had become clear to the owners that the structure needed a major renovation if it was going to continue to attract patrons. In 1984, this renovation was undertaken and, since renovations is known to ghost researchers to cause dormant spirits to stir, it was then that the ghostly activity first began to be reported.

Marilyn's Still Perfecting Her Craft...

Of all the ghosts in the Hollywood Roosevelt, by far the most famous is that of Marilyn Monroe. Her image is said to appear in a large mirror that used to hang in her room, but has since been moved to the hotel lobby.

How did this mirror become haunted? Actually, stories of haunted mirrors are not uncommon, as there seems to be something about mirrors that opens up a doorway to the spirit world. However, the story behind the haunted mirror in the Roosevelt Hotel is particularly fascinating.

Marilyn Monroe stayed in the hotel while working on films. On one occasion, she stayed in Room 1200. She requested and received a large mirror. Unknown to many of her fans, Marilyn Monroe took her acting career very seriously. She wanted the mirror because she used it to perfect her acting techniques. As she practiced her lines for whatever film she was working on, she would stand in front of the mirror and repeat the words and her body movements until she got things exactly right. She spent hours on end in front of the mirror, gazing into its surface.

After her death, the mirror was placed in the lobby. It wasn't long before hotel employees and patrons began to report seeing Marilyn's reflection looking back at them from the glass. In December 1985, about two months after the grand re-opening of the hotel, employee Suzanne Leonard was dusting the mirror. Looking into the mirror, she was shocked to see an image of an attractive blonde woman. She assumed that somebody had somehow crept into the room and turned around, however, nobody was there. She looked back into the mirror and could still see the reflection, which then slowly began to fade.

At first she didn't recognize the face. However, she soon learned that the mirror had, in fact, belonged to Marilyn Monroe. Ever since then, numerous other visitors have allegedly seen her reflection.

Brian Sapir has conducted Haunted Hollywood Tours for several years. One of his stops along the tour includes the Roosevelt Hotel. He says that he, along with tour patrons, have had many paranormal experiences there, including with Marilyn Monroe. "There was a guy on my tour who took a picture of the mirror that once decorated Marilyn's room…he took like five pictures and he got an image of Marilyn Monroe in his photographs," says Sapir.

Today the mirror remains in the hotel lobby, next to the elevator and the hotel gift shop. According to some sources, Marilyn Monroe's spirit has also occasionally been seen in the main ballroom.

Is Clift at the Hotel for Eternity?

Aside from Marilyn, the next most famous ghost in the Roosevelt is probably Montgomery Clift. In 1953, he spent three months living in Room 928 on the ninth floor while filming the blockbuster film "From Here to Eternity." During this time, he would stay either in his room or would wander the corridor outside his room, practicing his lines or playing on the bugle. He died tragically at the age of forty-six. The official cause of death was a heart attack.

After the renovation in 1984, Room 928 began to earn a reputation as a haunted room. Numerous guests complained of phantom footsteps, weird cold spots, sounds of bugle playing, and even invisible hands tugging at their clothes and bed sheets. Hotel maids also became puzzled by one particularly bizarre detail: the phone in the room would often be found off the hook, as if whoever was staying there didn't want to receive any calls...except there was nobody in the room!

Cocktail waitress Teryl Valazza is one of many hotel employees who has encountered Montgomery Clift's ghost. She says:

"I was getting off the ninth floor elevator, and I was walking down the hall, and I heard footsteps behind me. I turned around to see if there was anybody following me and there was nobody there. And as I continued to walk, I felt a cold breeze walk right by me. I went down in the elevator and never went back up."

In November 1992, a very shaken-up hotel guest was staying in the room with her husband when she felt an invisible hand pat her shoulder while she was reading in bed. Thinking it was her husband, she turned...only to find him sound asleep.

By this time, the fact that the actor's ghost haunted Room 928 was well known and was beginning to attract ghost hunters and other interested parties. In 1992, world-famous psychic Peter James stayed in the room. James says that he woke up at 3:30 a.m. to feel a sensation of a heavy weight laying on his body. He fell back to sleep, but woke up an hour and a half later at 5 a.m. — and a man was standing next to his bed! Incredibly shocked at the time, James says:

> "I realized that it was Montgomery Clift. He stood there for a few moments, walked over to the chair, and 'sat' there for approximately thirty minutes. He spoke of a very tormented life...He was a gentle soul with a boyish nature."

According to James, Clift's spirit then stood up, walked into the bathroom, and disappeared.

For those who doubt that Clift's ghost is still on the premises, they might want to hear what happened to a visiting hotel guest only a few years ago. Says hotel security agent Bruce Campbell, "She asked for the haunted room. Then, when she was trying to sleep, the coffee pot went on and off, the TV set started changing channels by itself, and the lights flickered on and off. She called downstairs and so we gave her a different room and the same thing happened like it followed her or something. She got so upset that she checked out about 4:00 a.m."

As Campbell assisted the upset guest check out of the room, he learned that she had tried to contact Montgomery Clift's spirit using a ouija board.

Marilyn Monroe and Montgomery Clift are among the Roosevelt Hotel's most famous ghosts, but they certainly aren't the only ones. There are, of course, unconfirmed reports of several other movie stars. Carol Lombard's spirit supposedly still haunts the luxury penthouse suite and Rudolph Valentino's apparition has been reportedly seen wandering the hotel corridors.

Swarming with Spirits...

However, this is just the beginning of the haunting activity occurring at this location. The hotel appears to have just as many dead guests as living ones, and not all of these ghosts are necessarily famous. Hotel employees have reported seeing an intimate couple dancing alone on the ballroom floor, apparently oblivious to their surroundings. The couple is seen moving across the dance floor one minute, and then the next minute, they are gone. Other employees have said that they heard ghostly music and sounds of activity coming from the dance floor. There are also numerous accounts of people who have seen little balls of lights that dance along the walls and disappear.

The main ballroom, or Blossom Ballroom, is the location of much of this activity. One of the most bizarre and persistent manifestations in this area is a cold spot located near the center. Researchers have measured it at about thirty inches in diameter. The air in this tightly defined circle has been repeatedly measured at about ten degrees cooler than outside the circle. Yet, no cause — such as air-conditioning vents or windows — can be found. It was first felt in December 1985. Alan Russell, personal assistant to the General Manager of the hotel, was sweeping the floor of the Blossom Room when he felt the extremely cold spot.

Later, a psychic was brought into the ballroom and said that he believed the spirit of a man dressed in black was causing the cold spot. However, he was unable to ascertain the identity of this mystery spirit.

Brian Sapir of Haunted Hollywood Tours says that he believes the cold spot may be the result of a murder that allegedly occurred in the hotel. Says Sapir, "In the late 20s and early 30s, [the hotel] was a major mafia hangout. And these guys that were working for the mob would often get together, do some gambling, and get drunk. When they got really high late at night, obviously they began some fights and arguments. And there were a couple of the gangsters who were actually murdered in the hotel, down in the underground [basement]."

Sapir says that many of the staff has encountered the ghosts of these gangsters, who are believed to be named Gus and Anson.

"The two mafia guys; one is tall and slender, and one is short and stubby. And these guys are wise guys, and they're ghosts. And they can do things — *very dark things* — where people have been pushed by invisible hands, bumps in the night, booming [noises] on the rooftop. And also, the cold spot in the Blossom Room right above where these characters were hacked up, stabbed, their bodies dragged out to the streets, and dumped on the sidewalk. When a murder occurs, and it's a tragic murder and a harrowing killing, the spirits don't cross over immediately, and do have unfinished business. At least that's my experience that I have encountered at the Roosevelt," says Sapir.

The ghosts are well known among the staff who hear constant complaints from guests about loud talking in adjacent rooms that turn out to be unoccupied and voices in the hallways. Sapir says that while management has tried to cover up the activity, they have been forced to admit that it is really happening.

"They give out four or five page handouts that were written up — just reports of haunting that were at the hotel. They say that the witching hour is two or three o'clock in the morning. Rooms will become so cold that people can't stay in them. The sound or noise coming from the rooftop, like the Penthouse Suite where Clark Gable and Carol Lombard still supposedly haunt. Even Babe Ruth supposedly haunts the hotel. They hear banging, the bats banging on the roof, and they check out of the hotel. People just can't stay in the hotel. It's like you check in, and you check out," says Sapir.

The staff has, not surprisingly, encountered evidence of ghostly activity on many occasions. A common complaint is that lights are being turned on in locked rooms. In one case, a maid said a ghost physically pushed her into a supply closet. In another account, an employee was walking by an empty locked office when he heard the sound of a typewriter inside. In a third case, a maid was in the hotel basement when a hanging bedspread began to sway back and forth by itself. All of this activity has led to an abnormally high turnover rate for the staff, many of whom allegedly quit after only a few days.

The accounts don't stop here. One anonymous staff member says that she observed a little girl playing by herself in the lobby. As she watched, the child vanished right before her eyes. According to hotel security agent Bruce Campbell, one ghost that has been seen by many of the staff members and guests is known as "Caroline." The identity of the ghost is believed to be that of a little girl who (with her brother) escaped from their hotel room while their dad was on an errand and drowned in the hotel Jacuzzi. Her brother survived. Since then, staff members have seen the girl's spirit wandering in various locations on the hotel premises. She is most often seen in the hotel lobby and is always wearing a blue dress. Whenever she is approached, she instantly disappears.

On one incredible occasion that has now become hotel legend, the ghost of the little girl actually called up a hotel staff member using the house phone in the hotel lobby. Says Campbell, "The little girl picked up the phone and said to the [PBX] operator, 'I'm looking for my daddy. I can't find my daddy.'"

According to Campbell, the operator told the little girl to just wait there and that they would find somebody to help her. She got a security agent and told him to check it out. The security agent went to the lobby and discovered it was empty. He figured that the child must be loose in the hotel. He checked the lobby, ballroom, restaurant, and then the bar when the girl called back.

Again, the girl asked the operator, "Did you find my daddy?"

The operator said no and told the girl to remain in one place so they could help her. The girl said, "Well, I really want to play," and asked the hotel operator if she would play with her. When the operator declined, the girl replied, "You're ugly!" and hung up the phone.

At this point, the operator got on the radio and told the security agent that the girl was on the phone at the lobby right now and to bring her to the front desk. The security agent said, "That's impossible. There's nobody on that phone because I'm standing right next to it."

Staff member Manny Frias has worked at the Roosevelt for twenty years. One evening he saw a young boy playing in the Jacuzzi. Realizing it was strange for such a young boy to be playing there alone, he looked around for his parents. Seeing nobody, he looked back down at the Jacuzzi...only to discover that the boy was gone. There were no wet footprints either. He speculates that it may have been the spirit of the brother of the little girl who had drowned in the Jacuzzi.

The Hollywood Roosevelt has so many ghosts that researchers and staff have had trouble keeping track of them all. There are reports of a ghostly piano player in a white suit that stands on the balcony of the ballroom, an unknown African American cook that haunts the kitchen area, and an unidentified ghostly clarinet player has often been seen wandering the premises.

A Ghost Hunter's Experiences....

Ghost researcher Brian Sapir has had several people on his ghost tour claim to have experiences while visiting the Roosevelt. Sapir admits that he too has had several paranormal experiences, a couple of which were particularly dramatic.

On one occasion, he took his tour to the hotel to meet author George Hodel, who had just written a book about the infamous Hollywood homicide case known as the Black Dahlia. Sapir and his touring customers had just entered the hotel and were in the lobby when the event occurred.

"We were standing in front of the locked display. It was on the wall — one of those [glass] display cases that had all the daily activities on it. It said "*Black Dahlia Avenger*." I had my back turned towards it, and I was chatting about the hotel and all the hauntings, and when I turned around, I saw the locked glass display case open itself, unlocking itself of its own volition. Nobody had touched it. There were five or six people standing next to me. We were all a minimum of three or four feet away. And the metal door swung open right towards us, ever so slowly, but it opened all the way. And we were shocked. It was amazing. I couldn't think of anything but the Black Dahlia and that her spirit was with us that night in a very special way. It was amazing."

Sapir says that he and all the other observers were amazed by the event, which was clearly paranormal. While it was thrilling to see the display case open by itself, another experience Sapir had in the hotel turned out to be even more incredible.

There's a bar in the hotel where many leading Hollywood men used to hang out and drink. Some of the stars included Errol Flynn, David Niven, the Barrymores, and William Holden. Errol Flynn was known to jump behind the bar and mix up his own special concoctions for himself and his friends. It was at this notorious bar where Sapir had an incredible encounter with a ghost.

"I was in that bar and I ordered a drink. I had been sitting there for a just a few moments. The drink was right in front of me, and I was looking up at the television. And right out of the side of my eye in my peripheral vision, I was looking down and I actually saw the glass begin to move. Ever so slowly, but it started to move — and it was moving to the left towards the bartender who was on the other side of the bar. She was leaning over and kneeling down and grabbing a bottle of wine. And I looked down and I saw that glass just take off like a silver bullet. It shot down the counter as quick as could be and almost landed on her head. She had to really back down to avoid it. It just flew right at her, just sucked right into her direction. And she looked dead into my eyes and asked if I had just seen what happened."

The Woman from the 1940s...

There is no shortage of ghost stories at the Roosevelt. Another comes from southern California resident and ghost researcher Kayte Johnson. In the mid-1980s, Johnson was driving through Hollywood with her friend Susan when they decided to stop at the hotel to make a phone call.

Susan went up to the front desk and began to argue with the clerk about using the phone. Meanwhile, Kayte stood next to them and looked around the lobby, soaking up the atmosphere of the historic hotel. She had only been in the hotel a few minutes when she encountered what she believes was a ghost.

"I looked over towards the staircase and there was this woman in a peach chiffon dress... It was beautiful. You could tell that the material was just very soft and very flowing, and that if she walked away, it would just swish. She had a gold belt around her waist, and the bust was kind of a princess cut — it wasn't very low. The sleeves were angel-wing sleeves...and I thought, 'Wow, you don't see that anymore.' Blond hair with all these short curls all over her head, and her jewelry — she looked like she was right out of the forties...She wasn't transparent. She was standing there looking at the foyer area, and I thought, 'Wow, that's very interesting.' I was thinking to myself, 'She can carry this off, like back in the '40s,'" says Johnson

So impressed and surprised by the appearance of this lady was Johnson that she turned to Susan and said, "Wow, you should do your hair like that."

Susan, who had been thinking of changing her hairstyle, turned and asked Kayte, "Do my hair like what?"

"Like that woman over there," Kayte said, pointing towards the staircase. There was nobody there.

Kayte looked around quickly, but the young lady was nowhere to be seen. "Where is that woman that was just standing there on the staircase with the peach-colored chiffon? She was like right out of the forties. Does she live here, or is she staying here?"

At this point the hotel clerk's eyes widened and she replied, "No, she's the resident ghost. She was a starlet many years ago. She played in several films."

Unfortunately, the clerk was unable to remember her name. However, Kayte was amazed. The lady looked as solid and normal as a living person. Kayte asked the clerk if there were other ghosts in the hotel. The clerk admitted that there were several, and told the story of a cab driver who was killed by a jealous husband back in the 1940s. The husband ran over the cab driver with his car, snapping his neck. Since then, many people have seen the cab driver's ghost hanging around the hotel.

As you can see, the Roosevelt is literally teeming with ghosts. According to some researchers, an estimated thirty-five ghosts inhabit the hotel. Likely, there are many more, making it one of the most haunted hotels — and one of the best places in the Greater Los Angeles to see a ghost....

"She had a little flower dress. She was about nine years old... She was very real. She was not transparent. She just simply did not come out of that ride. It made me feel a little crazy."

Chapter Two

Spirits of Universal Studios

100 Universal City Plaza
Universal City, CA 91608

Universal Studios was originally built in order to make movies, but is today also a popular theme park in Los Angeles. The park attracts thousands of people each year who enjoy the various rides and attractions related to the making of blockbuster movies. Unknown to many, however, is that the park is also *very* haunted.

Syd Schultz has worked at Universal Studios for many years, and he is also currently co-director of the Pasadena Paranormal Research Society, a professional ghost hunting organization. Part of the reason for his interest in ghosts is because of his incredible experiences with and research into ghostly manifestations at Universal Studios.

One of his most amazing experiences occurred around 1999. He was still a new employee, learning how to operate one of the rides, and says Schultz, "It was a very slow day. I was being trained at the facilities, and there were only two people in line to get on this ride. So we got them on [the ride] and sent them down the hallway. We have camera monitors because we can't see around the corner. Then on the cameras, this little girl shot past. She went running down the hallway… She was on a mission to get on the ride. She knew where she was going...like she belonged to that couple and was just left behind for a couple seconds. She had like a little flower dress. She was about nine years old. I got on the intercom, and I was telling these folks, 'Hey, be prepared. There's a little girl coming.' And then she proceeded to turn right into the room where they were already in. And then I got back on the intercom to let them know that she was already there. Well, the co-worker came out with his hands in the air, saying, 'What little girl?'

"So I waited for the ride to end. The couple got off — with *no* little girl — and of course, I was scratching my head. She was very real. She was not transparent. She just simply did not come out of that ride. It made me feel a little crazy in trying to explain it to myself."

Shocked, Schultz looked to his co-workers for an explanation. At first he assumed that the little girl was still lost somewhere on the ride. That's when one of his co-workers sat him down and told him the truth.

He said, "Okay, you've seen her."

Intrigued, Schultz replied, "I've seen who?"

"You've seen the little girl," his co-worker said. "She's very prominent around here at night."

Schultz learned that the girl had actually died while on the ride. At first, it was believed that the ride might have caused her death, but an autopsy later revealed that the girl had actually died of a brain aneurysm. Ever since then, she's made regular appearances. Her ghost manifests not only on the ride where she died, but also all across the park.

"I'm not going to give her name. Because of the family, it's being kept a secret, but she's very prominent in the park — and she does like to play… It's one of those things that's not hidden," Schultz said.

Schultz was amazed by his encounter. He began to ask around, and learned that several other employees had also seen the little girl's ghost. Several security guards, in particular, have seen her wandering around.

"They were driving from the upper to the lower lot. It's a long and winding road. They've actually seen the little girl up on the bridge waving down to them. He backed up the car and the little girl was gone. She's been seen running up and down the Star-Way and the Back to the Future Ride," says Schultz.

Though amazed by his encounter with the ghost of the little girl and all the other people's stories of their encounters, Schultz soon learned that the ghost of the little girl was only the tip of the iceberg. Soon his co-workers began to reveal that numerous other ghosts had also been encountered at the park.

"There are a lot of stories coming from the people who work there, especially from the night cleaners and maintenance people," says Schultz. "It's very interesting."

One incredible story that Schultz recounted involved a cleaning person who encountered the ghost of a little boy. Says Schultz, "She saw this little boy sitting on the ground. She said she tried to talk to him. The boy would not communicate, so she called security. Security went in and made the [cleaning] person call the supervisor. Well, the supervisor tried to get the answer to what they found out down there, and the security guard would not answer. He would not tell him. So finally, he had to call the other security guard, and that's when the head of security mentioned that the security guard had gone in, and the little boy looked up and disappeared right in front of him."

Apparently the security guard was so upset by the sudden disappearance of the child that he refused at first to discuss it. Later, Schultz learned more details about the ghost. "They said that he was wearing a two-piece, like a shirt and older-looking dirty jeans. [He wore] kind of hard-soled, older dress shoes."

Schultz learned that the boy had been seen on several other occasions and was apparently caught on one of the security video cameras. "They had on camera what was ectoplasm in the facility. When it came out of the wall, it set off the alarm because it was in a safe area in the facility. It kind of manifested, and you could see a hand and an arm, and it looked to be that of a small child, from the height," says Schultz.

The video was viewed by several of the security staff at the theme park, but as is standard practice, it was destroyed after ninety days.

Schultz has learned that several other areas in the park have earned a reputation for ghostly activity. Several of the prop houses reportedly have strange activity connected to the many different kinds of props. However, it is Stage 28 that has earned a particularly strong reputation for attracting ghosts.

"Several times I've been in that facility, and there's something just being inside that facility that gives you the feeling that somebody is there watching... Whatever is there likes to play pranks and tricks. It's very interesting," says Schultz.

It is this particular stage that is said to be haunted by the ghost of none other than horror icon, Lon Chaney. It was on this stage that he performed his most famous work, "Phantom of the Opera." Ever since his death, his spirit has reportedly been seen there, running along the catwalks. Writes researcher Cheri Sicard, "The caped figure of Lon Chaney is said to haunt Sound Stage 28 at Universal Studios (a bit of trivia you're not likely to hear on the tour). Several Universal employees have reported strange activities (apparitions, noises, cold spots) among the Jaws lagoon as well, especially after hours. The identity of this shade is unknown."

Other phenomena said to occur in Stage 28 include lights that turn on and off and doors that open and close by themselves.

Schultz has interviewed other employees who have their own stories to tell about ghostly encounters at Universal Studios. He is currently putting together a book about his investigations. He has discovered that the park was apparently built on an old battleground and that it had a strong Native American presence. Whatever the case, Schultz is convinced that Universal Studios is very haunted.

A Real Ghost for "Ghost Whisperer"...

Not surprisingly, Schultz is not alone in this belief. In fact, recently a series of unexplained events have occurred on the set of the hugely popular television program, "The Ghost Whisperer," starring Jennifer Love Hewitt. Numerous members of the crew and cast, including Jennifer Love Hewitt herself, claim to have had experiences.

In fact, Hewitt has been very forthcoming about some of the events she has experienced on the set of her show at Universal Studios. In 2006, a television journalist interviewed her and asked if she would discuss some of these experiences. Hewitt replied, "Sure. I think it's really cool and exciting and we've had all kinds of things happen. My makeup artist...we took a picture of her and she had sort of this white film over her face, then we took a picture of her ten minutes later in another part of the building and there was nothing."

They later had the photograph examined by well-known psychic medium James Van Praggh, who told them that the photograph definitely showed what he believed was a spirit.

Hewitt revealed other encounters.

"We've had lights explode. That's Jay Mohr's favorite story, because he's so excited that it was his head that it exploded over. Who in the world would be excited about glass exploding over their head? No one but Jay Mohr. He's very excited about that.

"And yeah, about the ghosts showing up? I've had them show up around me a lot on film. I think it's exciting. I think it's neat! And for people who don't believe, if it's sort of a weird coincidence, that's cool. And for people like me who do believe, I feel like we tell their stories every week. The spirits are really the stars of the show, and if they stop by to say, 'Hey, thanks,' and make an appearance every now and again, it's their show. They should! I think it's cool."

In an interview on the "TV Guide Channel," Hewitt revealed further details about some of the activity. "We've had lights move literally three and a half inches to the left. As you're sitting there, the lights move. We've had lights burst over actors' heads when they're playing people who don't believe in ghosts. A light will burst into a million pieces over them. People are like, 'We're not guest-starring on that show!' But for us, as a crew, we're kind of like, 'Awesome, maybe they're with us!'"

While appearing on the "Ellen DeGeneres Show," Hewitt talked some more about the paranormal happenings on the set and then played one of the video segments of apparent ghostly activity taking place. The film is just a short segment, but it clearly shows some sort of dark shadow moving behind Hewitt as she performs her scene.

"This just showed up on the footage, and the editor like came up with chills on his arms and was like, 'I need somebody else to tell me that they're seeing this also.' Seconds before that on the footage of the dailies, it's not there and it's not there afterwards. It was just there for that fleeting moment," says Hewitt.

The ghosts at Universal Studios may be attracted to the set of "Ghost Whisperer" for the simple fact that the show itself is about ghosts. Whatever the case, the activity is still ongoing. In September 2007 there was a strong "paranormal presence" on the set, which was experienced by numerous cast and crewmembers.

As Hewitt revealed in an interview with Kris DeLeon in the *World Entertainment News*, "There can be energies and spirits in and around places. We were filming in a certain part of the lot, and there was this building I was walking out of to start a scene, and there were seven crewmembers who went inside this building and had very strange experiences. One of the ladies felt her sweater being tugged and she couldn't explain it. Another guy felt somebody tugging on the bottom of his jeans—and I had the bottom of my dress tugged. We definitely felt something was in there."

As you can see, Universal Studios is still actively haunted and will likely remain that way for a long, long time. Why is this area so active? Unfortunately, any answer at this time would be mostly speculation. However, like other heavily haunted locations, Universal Studios has a long and colorful history. Many events involving intense human activities have taken place there over a long period of time. Some of the hauntings appear to be the result of a tragic, sudden death. Others might be better qualified as a "residual haunting." Whatever the explanation, the area is a prime spot in the Los Angeles area where anybody can go and possibly see an actual ghost.

Chapter Three

A Haunted Hospital

"You're not going to include the name of the hospital, are you?" The witness spoke pleadingly. She was a nurse at a major hospital in the eastern end of the San Fernando Valley.

"If you don't want me to, I won't," I told her, "but I'd like to."

"Well, you can't."

"Why?" I asked.

"The hospital is haunted!"

The witness explained that she was afraid that not only would the hospital supervisors become upset if they learned that the events at their hospital had been publicized, she was also worried that the stories would scare the patients, some of whom might decide not want to stay at the hospital. The only way she would agree to tell her story is on the condition that the hospital would not be named. She also insisted on remaining anonymous. I agreed, on the condition that I could name the general location of the hospital. A deal was struck, and the witness began her story.

I'll call her Brenda Sloan. Brenda, a single parent, had worked her way through school and had been working as a nurse for several years through the mid-1990s. She enjoyed her position at the hospital. She was assigned to the telemetry floor. Many of the hospital patients were hooked up to various machines that recorded their vital signs, such as heart rate and blood pressure. These machines are called telemetry boxes. It was Brenda's job, along with a small group of other nurses, to monitor the telemetry boxes and to respond to any emergency that might arise. For example, suddenly one of the viewing screens might show a serious drop in blood pressure. An alarm would go off and the nurses would have to spring into action.

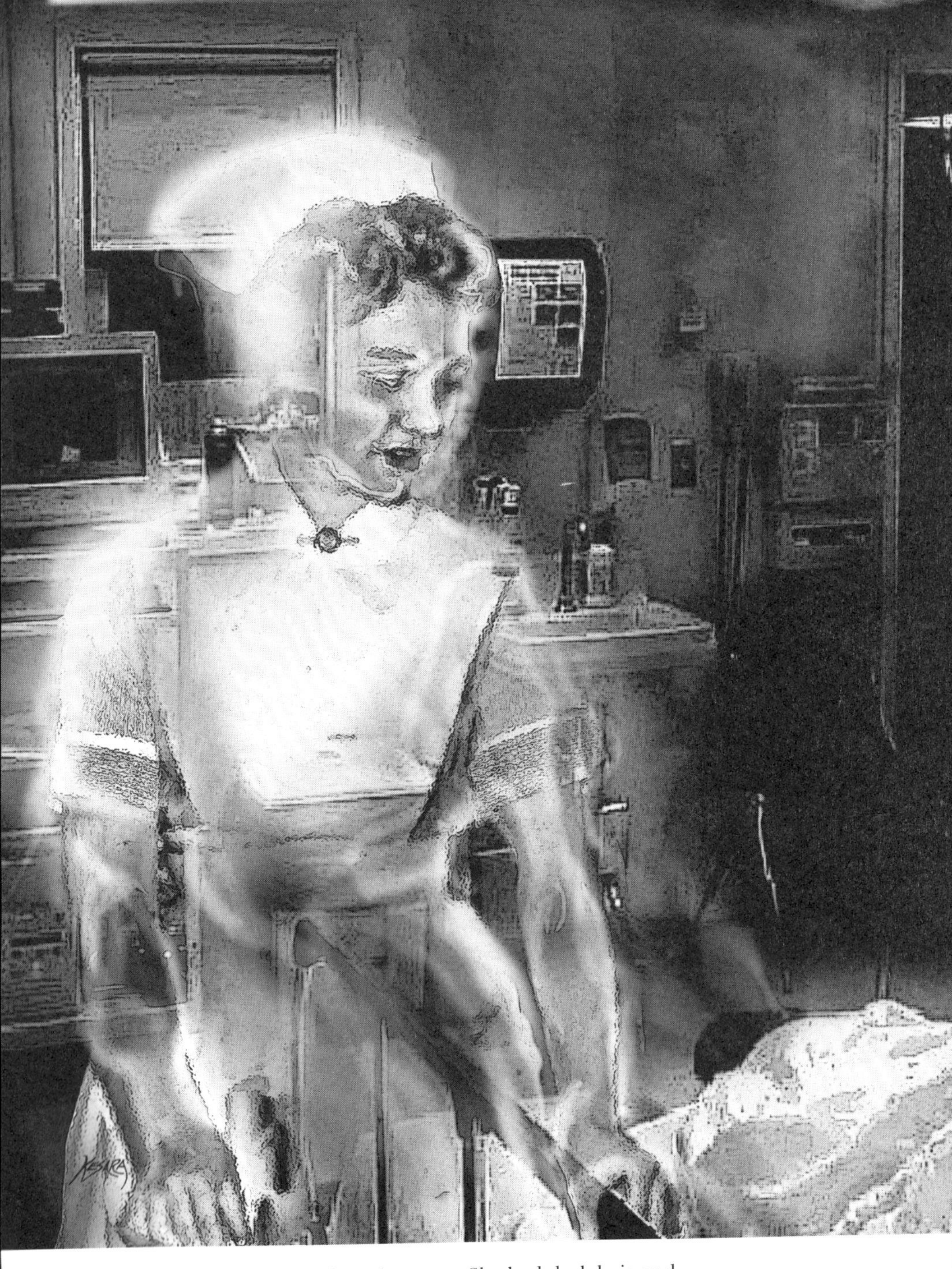

"This nurse would come into the room. She had dark hair and was wearing an older nurse uniform with a white hat…the only problem was, none of the nurses wore white hats."

Brenda liked the job, but it wasn't long after she started that she was warned about the ghost on the telemetry floor. "This is what they told me on the night shift, because we'd sit around and talk and it would be kind of eerie late at night, because it's a real big hospital. And the hospital charge nurse — actually several nurses — told us that up on the telemetry floor, they'd see a box go off. All of a sudden, the telemetry monitor wouldn't be on. And they would go into the room, and they'd say to the patient, 'Where's your box at?' And the patient would point and it would be up on a shelf. Now these are patients who are bedridden, who can't get up and put their telemetry box up on a shelf, you know what I mean?

"And the nurse would say, 'Who took this off you?' The patient would say, 'Well, the nurse did, the one with the white hat on.' The only problem was, none of the nurses wore white hats. And the description of the nurse didn't match any of the nurses who worked there at that time. She appeared to be an older woman with dark hair, wearing an old-fashioned uniform with a white hat."

The first time it happened, the nurse who came into the room just assumed that the patient had somehow disconnected the telemetry himself. She retrieved the box and hooked the patient up again, not thinking too much about it.

However, it wasn't long before it happened again. The monitor technician shouted out to her that the telemetry box in the same room had gone off. The nurse rushed into the room, which was now occupied by a different patient. She entered and saw that the box was missing. She looked up on the shelf — the box was placed in exactly the same position it had been put in the first time. She looked at the patient and asked, "Why is your box off?"

The patient said, "Well, another nurse came in and took it off me and put it up here."

Shocked, the nurse re-connected the machine and told the other nurses what had happened. It was then that they began to wonder if they had a ghost on their hands.

Not long after that, it happened a third time. Then it started happening regularly, and to different nurses. It was always exactly the same. It would occur only on the night shift — and always in the same room.

"This nurse would come into the room. She had dark hair and was wearing an older nursing uniform with a white hat. And she would disconnect the telemetry box, put it up on a shelf, and leave," says Brenda.

Obviously, the situation was becoming dangerous. As news of the ghost spread, more and more nurses refused to be assigned to that room. After a tenth incident, the nurses decided to take action. A few of the nurses who had witnessed the incidents went together as a group to the night-shift hospital supervisor and asked to speak with him.

The supervisor looked at the nurses and asked them, "What is the problem?"

One of the nurses stepped forward and explained the situation. First she told him about the initial few incidents and then told him that it had now escalated to a point where it was becoming dangerous. She told him, "This keeps happening night after night, with patient after patient."

"And who do you think this nurse is?" he asked.

The nurses didn't hesitate with their answer. "We think she's a ghost...the ghost of a nurse who used to work here."

To their surprise, the supervisor believed them, and asked them what they thought should be done about the situation. They told him, "You need to bring a priest in here and have this hospital blessed."

Brenda isn't sure if the blessing ever took place, but the haunting continued either way. The same ghost began to appear more regularly and in different locations throughout the hospital, but particularly in front of the elevator on the fifth floor.

"A lot of times, we would be running errands in the hospital, and everybody hated it when the elevator would stop at the fifth floor, because they'd always see the nurse walking away in that white uniform with a white hat on. And the floor would smell like smoke. And back when that lady worked there, nurses used to go and smoke in the nurses' lounge. It would freak everyone out, because they'd get a glimpse of her. She'd be there, and then she wouldn't be. So they hated when the elevator doors would open on that floor. And several nurses said that," says Brenda.

So far, Brenda herself has not seen the ghost. However, she soon learned that the ghosts were not limited to the fifth floor. Another haunting was also taking place in the Neonatal Intensive Care Unit (NICU).

Brenda had worked in several different positions and, when she was assigned to the NICU, she was delighted. She loved babies and working with infant patients was particularly rewarding.

It wasn't long after she started working there, however, that strange things began to happen. At first it started with an eerie feeling that she was being watched. She'd be retrieving supplies or caring for a patient when she'd have the distinct feeling that someone else was in the room. On several of these occasions, she would see "little flashes" in her peripheral vision.

After several such incidents, she told one of her fellow nurses, who agreed that the NICU was definitely spooky. "We always felt like there were little people around us, little ghosts. We always had these weird feelings... That unit was just weird. It kind of tripped us all out. We'd always get weird kinds of feelings at night, like being watched or stared at, or seeing something out of the corner of your eye. There are certain rooms that you just feel like there is a presence," says Brenda.

One day Brenda was working at the NICU along with the charge nurse when a patient's mother came running out of the room holding her baby and said, "We can't stay here anymore!"

The charge nurse and Brenda looked at each other with raised eyebrows and then back at the patient's mother. "Why?" Brenda asked.

The mother replied, "Because a little girl keeps coming into our room. It's like she disappears before my eyes. She comes into the room, she goes up to my baby's crib, she looks in the crib, and she looks at me...and then she just disappears!"

The mother explained that she had woken up in the middle of the night and saw the little girl there, and then again at 6:30 in the morning, she woke up and saw the little girl come into the room — and disappear right before her eyes. She told Brenda and the charge nurse, "I want to go home. I don't want to stay here."

Brenda soon learned that this wasn't the only incident involving the little girl. Other patients had described the same exact thing, though nobody seemed to know who the ghost of the girl was.

"She was just normal looking, short brown hair, brown eyes... just a little girl. She was dressed in regular clothes. She wasn't in a hospital gown. She wasn't hooked up to an IV. She was just this little girl, probably about four years old," says Brenda.

Brenda and the other nurses would often sit and talk about the various incidents. She learned that many of them had experienced paranormal activity. Some of the nurses said that they had also experienced supernatural events at other hospitals where they had worked previously. They theorized that because so many people die in the hospital, it's only a matter of time before they all become haunted to some degree.

On one occasion, they were discussing some recent paranormal events when the hospital nurse manager came in and overheard their discussion. He joined their group and began to listen with interest. When they were done, he sat down and told them that ghosts were no laughing matter. He explained that as nurses, their jobs would involve dealing with death, and that there was always the possibility that something supernatural might happen. He told them that he believed their stories, and then said that he had some important advice to share with them about how to deal with their unique situation. "He said, 'Whenever you lose a patient — whenever you have a patient die — never go straight home because you don't want the spirit attached to you. Go to a grocery store, or go somewhere else where there are lots of people before you go straight home,'" says Brenda.

Brenda and the other nurses were shocked that their supervisor took the subject so seriously, but he explained that supernatural activity had become a problem for several of his nurses on prior occasions and he had learned how to deal with it.

Brenda says that while she was a little "freaked out" by all the activity, she also learned to deal with it. Then later she received an outstanding career opportunity to work at another medical facility in nearby Simi Valley. The offer included a large sign-on bonus and was too good to refuse. Brenda accepted the job and began her new job at the new hospital.

Brenda was relieved that she would no longer have to deal with all the strange activity that was taking place at her old workplace. She soon learned, however, that the other nurses were right — pretty much all hospitals are haunted. It wasn't long after she started her new job that she began to experience strange activity. Again, Brenda insists that the hospital's name remain anonymous.

Her first experiences occurred in labor room number four. Every time she entered the room, she felt like somebody was watching her. The feeling of some kind of presence was distinct and strong. She mentioned it to her co-workers, and soon learned that many of them had the same feelings and believed the room was haunted.

The room is the last room along a hallway. It used to be an ER, but was converted into a labor room. Brenda soon learned to dread working in the room. "Labor Room Four...we've always known about it. All these strange things happen in there whenever you do a delivery. It's like you have to triple check everything, because what can go wrong will go wrong in that room. You'll go to bag and mask somebody, and you'll put out the bag, and there will be no mask on it. You'll go to suction somebody, and all of a sudden your suction won't work, or something is gone. It's just crazy, that room. That's Labor Room Four. I can't stand it," says Brenda.

Brenda learned to deal with the strange activity and "weird stuff," but she didn't like it. She did get some measure of relief, however, to know that she wasn't the only one having to deal with it. On one occasion, even her supervisor had an experience.

When the room wasn't being used, the hospital staff often used it to take their breaks, eat their lunch, or take a nap. Says Brenda, "My boss was lying in there taking a nap, and she kept hearing strange noises, and feeling like a pressure on her. And my boss doesn't believe in this stuff. She came bolting out of the labor room and said, 'There something in there! I feel weird in there. I can't be in there! It's weird.'"

Brenda looked at her in amazement and, knowing how conservative her boss was about the supernatural, she told her, "Oh, my God, you are saying that."

Her supervisor replied, "Yeah. I felt weird. I felt like something was on me. I heard noises. I can't be in there."

Just recently, a new hospital employee was assigned to cleaning up Labor Room Four. Brenda knew it was only a matter of time before the orderly would experience something — and she was right. The orderly had only been working there a few weeks. One day she was in Labor Room Four, cleaning it up, when Brenda saw her come running out of the room in fear. She rushed up to Brenda with wide eyes and told her, "Senora, that room is crazy!"

Brenda replied, "I know!" and told her that weird things happen in there.

The orderly shook her head. "No, no. I'm in there. I'm cleaning the bathroom. I walk out to clean the sink. The door is shut. Then it flings open by itself, and there's nobody there! Nobody!"

"I know," Brenda repeated. "I was waiting for something to happen to you in there."

Again, Brenda insisted that the name of the hospital be anonymous, but she says that from what she has learned, her experiences are not unique. Because of the nature of hospitals, she believes that many, if not all of them, are haunted. So next time you are visiting one of these institutions, in Los Angeles or elsewhere, remember that if you are lucky (or unlucky if you are afraid of such things), you just might have an encounter with a ghost.

Chapter Four

A Last Goodbye

As any ghost researcher will tell you, just about any location can become haunted. Hotels, houses, roadways, cemeteries, theaters...all are vulnerable to ghosts. Ghost researchers also agree that objects can also be haunted. Antique objects, sacred artifacts, musical instruments, and mirrors...these are the types of objects to which ghosts sometimes connect themselves. Today some researchers have now come to the conclusion that even people can become haunted.

The phenomenon of poltergeists has been very well documented, with literally hundreds of recorded cases. These provide the perfect example of hauntings that seem to be centered on a person rather than a location. In these cases, the ghostly activity follows a familiar pattern and often involves the presence of an emotionally disturbed adolescent or, in some cases, an adult.

One theory to explain poltergeists is that the energy that causes the paranormal activity is actually coming from a living person — the disturbed adolescent — who is causing the activity on an unconscious level. Another theory is that evil, non-human spirits — demons — are responsible. A third theory that is growing in popularity is that some poltergeist cases are the result of uncontrolled mediumship. In this theory, the person having the experience is not disturbed in any way, but is rather attracting ghosts who want to communicate.

"I looked down the hallway and there was this huge sparkling circle of light. It made this humming noise and it just felt like energy. It was beautiful. It came down the center of the hall."

Some people, for an unknown reason, appear to be born with the ability to sense and communicate with ghosts. The case of Matthew Manning, a young man from England, provides a typical example. From a young age, a wide variety of intense poltergeist phenomena plagued Manning wherever he went. The problem became so pervasive that he had to be removed from his school.

However, later, as an adult, Manning became an influential and powerful psychic medium. He says that as a child, he was the center of so much paranormal activity because the spirits — knowing he could hear them — were attempting to communicate with him.

Whether or not this explains all poltergeist cases is hard to say. However, ghost researchers now recognize that some people are more likely than others to encounter ghosts. We call these people mediums because they are able to sense the presence of ghosts when most people cannot.

Brenda Sloan, who works as a nurse at a major Los Angeles area hospital, does not call herself a medium and would probably disagree with anybody who did. However, she does admit to having had an abnormally large number of ghost encounters and says that for some reason she seems to be the focus of a lot of activity.

As in other similar cases, it began in her childhood and continues to the present day. As a child, Brenda would often sense — *and sometimes actually see* — a strange dark apparition, which she found frightening, particularly because on rare occasions, it felt like it was trying to possess her.

"I used to feel it at the house I lived in. I would see it, and I would shield my eyes and look away. And a couple of times, I would feel the pressure of it when I was sleeping. It was a dark presence," says Brenda.

In her late twenties, Brenda became pregnant. It was during her pregnancy that she again began to be visited by spirits. Unknown to Brenda, when a woman becomes pregnant, her chances of being visited by a spirit increases dramatically. Some ghost researchers believe that the reason for this is because spirits are watching over the mother and soon-to-be-born child.

Whatever the reason, several researchers have noticed this connection. For Brenda, however, it came as a complete surprise. "I was probably four to six months pregnant. I was laying in bed and I just had this feeling to turn over. And I turned over and I looked...and there was a lady. She was probably about 5'7", but only the top of her showed. She had short gray hair, light eyes, and a nice pleasant smile, and she was standing there smiling over me. I looked up and focused on her face, and she just kind of evaporated from the bottom up and was gone."

Although the visitation was shocking and unexpected, it was also very comforting. Brenda did not recognize the lady, but says that she seemed very friendly. The encounter was not frightening, but instead was very positive.

About two weeks later, she received another visitation from the same friendly and mysterious spirit. "I was on my way to work, and I turned around and she was in the back of my car! I was like, okay, I have a passenger," says Brenda.

Again, after a few moments, the apparition faded. And again, Brenda felt only comfort. She told a few people about it, and one person told her that it was her guardian angel. Brenda doesn't know if this is true, but she does admit that she saw the same ghostly lady twice. It was not, however, to be her last ghostly experience.

One of Brenda's most vivid encounters with a ghost occurred in her apartment in Canoga Park.

"I'll just tell you the whole story," says Brenda. "One day I was sitting down watching TV and out of my hallway came this tall bald-headed man. He had a very pleasant look on his face. He was kind of transparent, but you could see his face and the outline. But I didn't recognize him. And he walked past me, past my TV, and he sat down in my living room chair and just sat there! And I'm like, 'Okay, this will go away. This is just going to go away.' I was like, 'whoa!' I couldn't even watch TV. I looked over at him, and he's just sitting there. I was like, am I seeing this? I had to do a double take."

After a few moments, the apparition faded away, though Brenda wondered if the apparition was still there, but she just couldn't see it. While the experience was disconcerting, Brenda says that she wasn't afraid. The ghost seemed very benevolent and she did not feel threatened by his presence at all, but still she had questions. Who was he? Why was he in her apartment?

A few weeks later, she went to have dinner at a friend's house. She was sitting at the kitchen table when a woman she'd met only once before came up to her and said, "There's a tall bald man behind you with red hair. He said his name is Ben."

Unknown to Brenda, the woman who told her this also had some mediumistic abilities. It was the specificity of the name and description that caught her attention. "That's my grandfather!" she blurted out.

The woman said, "Well, he says hello, and he's going to be here until you are finished. He's watching over you until you get things done."

"I was blown away!" Brenda says, adding that she now believes that the apparition of the man she saw in her living room was probably her grandfather, whom she never met in person and therefore had trouble recognizing.

Later, tragedy struck Brenda's life when her good friend died. Around the same time, paranormal activity in her apartment began to occur. This time, her son Christopher (not his real name) was also a witness.

"Christopher was standing in the kitchen and I was sitting on the couch. I had a pair of shoes sitting in the kitchen. And the shoes — simultaneously and still together — slid about four feet across the floor. I looked up at Christopher and he looked at me, and I said, 'Did you see that?'" says Brenda.

"He said, 'Yes, I did, mom.' And he came and ran and jumped on the couch. I just got up and put the shoes back where I had them. And I said, 'Don't touch my shoes!' It was really weird."

Around this time, tragedy struck Brenda's life again when another friend of hers died. In this case, her friend Karen (not her real name) died while giving birth to a baby. Although overcome with grief, Brenda decided she had to help Karen's husband care for their newborn child and went to stay over at their house until Karen's grieving widow could get back on his feet. Brenda was, of course, deeply saddened by the tragedy. However, almost as soon as she arrived, she began to see Karen's apparition moving around the house, watching over both her and the baby.

"I would be in the kitchen doing the dishes and cleaning, and I'd look down the hall... I always saw her peeking out of the baby's room, looking at me and smiling. It used to freak me out," says Brenda. "I saw her all the time. She'd always be just looking out and smiling at me. I'd see her long hair flowing back in and out of the room, and I just kind of pretended that I didn't see it. I just didn't know what to think!"

On another occasion, she was vacuuming the floor when she came upon a pair of Karen's shoes. She picked up the shoes and put them outside. She then returned to the vacuum, turned around...and got an incredible shock: the shoes were back in the same place! By this point, she had become somewhat used to the unusual activity and just said, "Oh, well."

According to Brenda, "None of it fazed me."

The visitations from her friend Karen came to a climax one evening when Brenda was sleeping on the couch next to the baby. She woke up because she suddenly felt this strange pressure coming down on her body. Says Brenda, "It was like she was lying on top of me. I said, 'You've got to get off of me! You've got to get off!'"

After a few moments, the strange pressure lifted. Brenda is convinced that it was Karen trying to get her attention again, adding, "It was the weirdest thing."

Brenda went back to sleep. However, later in the night she woke up to one of the most fantastic experiences of her entire life. The experience began with a strange noise that was coming from the hallway. Says Brenda:

"I could hear this buzzing, like a humming noise. It sounded like electricity. And I looked down the hallway, and there was this huge sparkling circle of light. It was almost like a million dots of white light. It was clustered. And then they just kind of separated. As the circle got bigger, the little lights got farther apart. It made this humming noise and it just felt like energy. It was beautiful.

"It came down the center of the hallway and kind of hugged the wall. And then it came into the living room and it went up along the top part of the wall. I was looking at it, and I was just blown away. And then it kind of went jing-jing-jing, and ricocheted off all the walls."

Brenda wasn't sure how she knew, but she was absolutely certain that what she was seeing was her friend Karen saying goodbye. "I felt it was her...I felt like it was her energy. And the feeling that it gave off — it wasn't a frightening thing. It was this really calm, but happy excitement — a happy feeling like, yahoo!!! I don't know how to explain it. It wasn't scary. It wasn't a bad thing," says Brenda.

After less than a minute of bouncing around the room, the cluster of lights that was Karen made a sudden and dramatic exit. "It just ricocheted — bling-bling-bling — off all of the walls. All the little lights stayed in a cluster, and when it started ricocheting, it seemed to get smaller. And then the humming stopped and it went away. And then I had this feeling like, 'It's okay,'" says Brenda.

Brenda admits that she has had other unusual experiences. One time in church, she saw a pair of glowing apparitions and, as we now know, she has also seen spirits at the hospitals where she works as a nurse *(see the Haunted Hospital)*. Thankfully for her, most of her experiences with spirits have been very positive and benevolent. Still, she admits that she doesn't like seeing ghosts, and that she doesn't talk much about it. It's a part of her life that, for now, remains largely a secret to those around her.

Chapter Five

Claudia's Ghosts

As we have seen, some people are more likely than others to see ghosts. Claudia Blacios, who lives with her husband and daughter in the Greater Los Angeles area, is one of those lucky — or unlucky, depending on your view — people. Ever since she was a young girl, she has had the ability to see spirits. Though she doesn't call herself a medium, she, like Brenda Sloan, does admit to having had an abnormally large number of ghostly experiences. For some reason, she says, she was always sensitive to these types of things.

"I remember it all started when we were very little and we were playing with the Ouija board. And it was horrible. I'll never play with those things again. I don't think we were talking to anything that was normal. It was just a really weird experience..." says Claudia. "As far as ghosts go, I've seen them...I've seen my dead grandfather. They look like regular people, but there's something different about them."

Shortly after she became a teenager, Claudia learned the hard way that some locations are more haunted than others and, for a person with mediumistic like herself, it can have unforeseen consequences.

"I stay away from hospitals, especially the emergency room," says Claudia, "and I stay away from cemeteries. Because something always follows me home. I've been going through this since I was fourteen. As soon as I hit puberty, I started to experience these things. I'd walk into a room...and a glass would shatter. I'd walk into the room...and the TV would go off. Sometimes I would walk past lights — like the Chevron Station signs — and they would burn out. Someone told me that that was a release of energy, and that's what doing those things."

"I remember it all started when we were very little. We were playing with the Ouija board, and it was horrible. I'll never play with those things again. I don't think we were talking with anything that was normal."

Claudia says that she noticed other strange things that seem to involve the same phenomenon. She has reluctantly come to realize that she has a poltergeist that is somehow attached to her.

"A lot of people thought I was crazy when I would tell them that things would happen, but if I'd sit at home and think about it hard enough, things would just happen. Just recently my husband was sitting on this bench, and he was making me very angry. He kept teasing me. I thought, 'Man, I'd just love to slap you!' And all of a sudden the bench broke and he fell over. And I was just thinking about hurting him when he actually got hurt. That was really funny!"

On several occasions, while sleeping at night, spirits that she can only sense in a state of "sleep paralysis" have visited Claudia. While a skeptic might assume that these were simply dreams and hallucinations, Claudia has reason to believe otherwise.

"I'll be falling asleep, and I'll be laying there and all of a sudden I cannot move. I can't scream. I feel like something's sitting on top of me and I'm just paralyzed — and I know if I open my eyes I'm going to go completely crazy if I see it. I know that there's something there," says Claudia.

Skeptics assume that cases like these can be explained away as sleep paralysis that involve purely illusory events. Claudia has experienced this strange state many times and was never completely sure if she was imagining things or not. Then one evening, she had her answer....

"I remember the weirdest encounter I ever had with that. Right before I had my daughter, a year after I got married, I was at home. It was about four o'clock in the morning and I couldn't fall asleep and I was watching videos. And I started falling asleep when I felt that coming on. And it kind of felt like it was as loud as the engine of an airplane ringing in my ears, and I was paralyzed. I couldn't move. I couldn't scream. I remember laying there, thinking, 'Oh, great! Not you again!'"

Claudia was not happy to hear the spirit start speaking to her. "It sounded like it was talking underwater, telling me, 'If you move, if you try to escape, I'm going to hurt you.' And it would scratch me, pull me, and yank the blankets off. And I remember laying there, thinking, 'Okay, okay, okay, I'm not going to try to move. You can stay here as long as you need to be here, but can you turn up the TV...I really like that song!"

At the time of the incident, Claudia was watching a video featuring C & C Music Factory. To her surprise, the spirit obeyed her command and physically turned up the volume on her television!

"All of a sudden, the TV got really loud. And I said, "Wait a minute. That's too loud. My neighbors are going to start banging on the walls.' And all of a sudden, I hear bang-bang-bang-bang from the people next door. And all of a sudden, the volume goes back down. And that was the first time it was actually moving things in my house. It did something to the TV."

Thankfully, Claudia has learned how to control her connection to the spirit world.

"I learned how to beat it. If I'd try to scream, I couldn't. Its hand was so big that when it would try to cover my mouth that it would cover almost my whole face and I could not breathe," says Claudia, "and now, I know when it's coming. I feel it coming even before it's close to me and I would wake up. And I would say, 'No, you're not going to get me today. I'm not going to let you.' I can do that now, but back then, I couldn't. The attacks, they still happen, but not as frequently."

Claudia says that despite all her precautions, she still attracts numerous spirits. "Those kinds of things still happen. I still see things come through the house, and things follow me home. I go to the cemetery and visit my husband's dead uncle. And I'm thinking, 'Okay, who's going to come home with me today.' And sure enough, when I get home, the TV will go on and off, and there'll be some activity in the house for a while. Things will be on the table and then they'll be somewhere else, and no one touched them. And that will go on for a couple of days, but eventually they leave. I tell them, 'Go home. You're dead. You need to leave, cross over. And they go.' And now, it's like I'm stronger. I can control those bursts of energy. I can sometimes do it at will. Now it's not such a hassle."

Claudia has also had many profound psychic experiences. Once, as a child, she was caught ditching class. She was about to face the teacher when she thought to herself, "I wish there would be an earthquake!" Less than ten minutes later, as the teacher was walking up to her, an earthquake struck. Needless to say, the teacher ran for safety and Claudia escaped punishment.

Claudia has had other weird experiences with earthquakes. For two weeks in January 1994, Claudia kept dreaming about earthquakes. Each evening she would wake up. Finally, the Northridge earthquake hit on Martin Luther King Day.

She has also had many other psychic experiences, such as telepathy and clairvoyance, which she feels are somehow connected to her poltergeist. While sometimes it can be exciting, it also has a dark side, which leaves her somewhat ambivalent.

"It's fun when you can do things, but when you have to take the bad with it, the bad is bad. So a lot of the times, I feel like, 'Why is God doing this to me? Why me? Why can't I be like everybody else who never sees any of this stuff, that goes through life and everything's normal?'" says Claudia.

Claudia learned that her grandfather and her uncle and aunt also had problems with spirits who would appear to them and follow them. She speculates that her situation might be somehow genetically inherited. Whatever the case, she has learned to live with the fact that she has weird experiences.

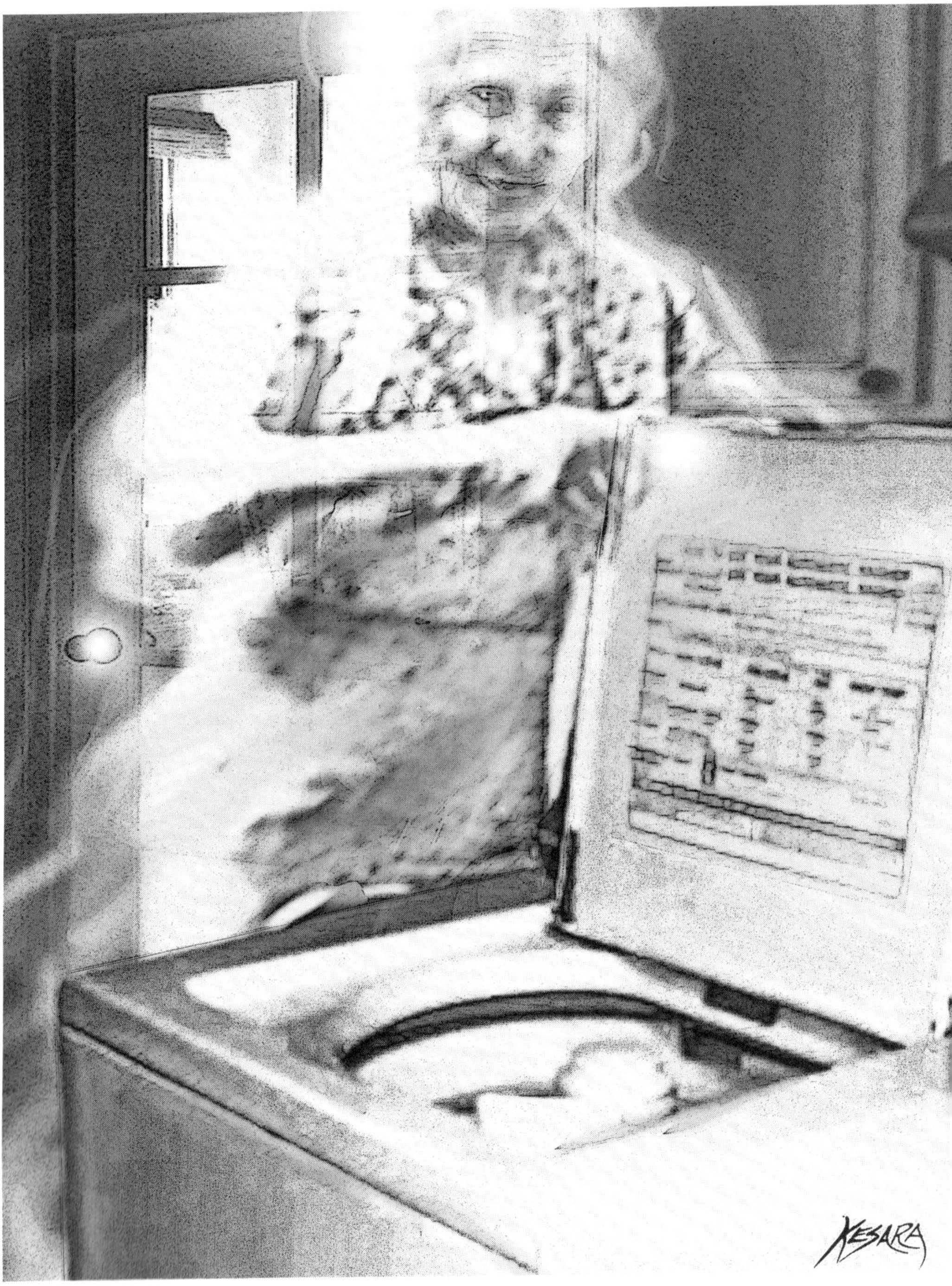

"She felt a presence behind her. She turned to her head to look and was surprised to see this 'little elderly woman' standing right behind her... She had an angry expression on her face."

Chapter Six

A Haunted Laundry Room

There is no need to fear ghosts. They are only people, just like you and I, but for one reason or another, they have become attached to the physical world. While some hauntings can continue for decades, others can be easily resolved by simply communicating with the ghost, as in the following case.

In this instance, the first sign of anything unusual began when a middle-aged married couple bought a home in Woodland Hills, California. The wife, Shelly (pseudonym), was an elementary school teacher. It wasn't long after they moved in that she learned that their house was haunted. Bizarrely, the activity seemed to be limited only to the laundry room and only involved the clothes washing machine.

When they moved into the house, Shelly was excited to have a laundry room, which she installed with modern new machines. The clothes washer was a top-loader design, meaning it had a lid on the top that opened and closed.

It was after she did the laundry each week that Shelly was confronted with a bizarre mystery. After she took the laundry out of the washer and put it into the dryer, she would close the lid of the washer. However, each time she came back into the room, the lid would be open.

The first few times this happened, she didn't think much of it, assuming that she must have forgotten to close the lid. However, after it happened several more times, she realized it couldn't be mere forgetfulness. To verify this, she made a point to make sure that she kept the lid closed after she used the machine.

When she returned back to the room after doing the laundry, she was not surprised to see that the lid was back up. Shelly was then certain that something very strange was going on in her laundry room. The only explanation she could think of was that a ghost haunted the room. But who, she wondered? And why would they keep opening the lid to the clothes washer? None of it made any sense.

Shelly told her husband who was at first skeptical. However, he soon learned that his wife was not lying. The strange mystery continued for several months. No matter how many times they closed the clothes-washer, when they returned...the lid would be opened. They *never* saw it move. They *never* heard any strange noises. It only happened when nobody was in the room.

Neither of them had any idea who was doing it or why, but they speculated that it might be somebody who used to live in the house. The mystery remained, however: why disturb the washer and nothing else?

Then one day Shelly had an experience in the laundry room that solved the entire mystery. She was in the laundry room and had just transferred the clothes out of the washer and into the dryer. She then closed the lid to clothes-washer and, while looking at it, she felt a presence behind her. She turned her head and was surprised to see "this little elderly woman" standing right behind her. The woman was looking over Shelly's shoulder at the closed lid of the washer. She had an angry expression on her face...like she was mad at Shelly for closing the lid.

That's when Shelly had a revelation. Of course! she thought. She suddenly remembered that in the past, the older clothes-washers sometimes had a problem with mildew. If you didn't leave the machine open to air out, the bin would often grow mold or mildew. However, these machines were new, better designed, and had no such problem.

On an impulse, Shelly decided to communicate with the ghost. She said out loud, "This is the year 2002...you can close the lids on our washing machines. They don't get mildew."

The apparition slowly faded away. Shelly says that after this, she never again had a problem with the washing machine. A haunting that had gone on for several months was suddenly resolved by simply communicating with the ghost.

This experience caused Shelly to become interested in ghosts and she was eager to have another experience. She soon learned to regret this decision. She had heard there was a haunted hotel in the French Quarter in Louisiana, so she went there with her husband and asked for the most haunted room. They entered the room and, as her husband started putting away their belongings, Shelly decided to take out her camera and see if she could capture any strange images on film.

Shelly said that as soon as she began to take the first photograph, it felt like somebody smacked the camera right out of her hand. The camera flew completely across the room. Both Shelly and her husband looked at each other and then at the camera lying on the floor on the other side of the room. "Okay," Shelly said. It was obvious to both of them that the ghost was angry and did not want its picture taken.

Shelly thinks she must have angered the ghost because of what happened the next day. The first sign of trouble began as they were exiting the hotel. As soon as they were outside, someone or something pushed Shelly from behind, and she fell flat on her face on the cement. Her husband thought she was playing around, but Shelly told him that something just pushed her to the ground.

Shelly learned the lesson the hard way: that ghosts are just people — and it's not always a good idea to bother them.

"She looked totally solid. I thought it was somebody who had come in... She just looked at me like she was ignoring me, turned, and walked back into the front room. I walked in...and there was nobody there."

Chapter Seven

Augustine

Tony Tocco and his friend Mark were excited. They had just rented and moved into their new home in Inglewood. It was a nice neighborhood, mostly occupied by wealthy retired people who had worked at the nearby Northrup Aircraft Company. Their neighbors on either side were both retired.

The house was exactly what they were looking for: two bedrooms, a big yard, and quiet neighborhood. The only thing wrong with it was that it did need to be cleaned up and the yard was badly overgrown, but otherwise, it was perfect. As they had hoped, it was quiet and homey. Tony took one bedroom and his roommate Mark took the other.

They spent the first few days unpacking their stuff and setting up the house. It was during this time that Tony began to notice movement out of the corner of his eye. Each time he looked, however, nothing was there, so he didn't think anything of it.

On the third day, they were still cleaning up the house. Tony was working in the kitchen when Mark announced that he was going to the store to get some beer. Tony remained at the kitchen sink, cleaning. It was then that he had his first of what would become hundreds of encounters with a ghost. Says Tony, "Just after Mark left, I see this lady walk into my front room from the kitchen door, kind of out of the corner of my eye. She had dark hair, a little Mexican lady."

Tony jerked his head around and looked. Nobody was there. He shook his head and thought, "Must have imagined it."

The figure, however, had seemed so real, so detailed. He wondered if maybe Mark had come back in looking for his car keys or something, but finding nobody in the house, he just shrugged his shoulders and returned back to cleaning the kitchen. Then the lady appeared a second time.

"I had my back turned, and then I see her again. This time she walked into the kitchen and I turned — and as I turned and looked, she looked at me. I said, 'Hello, excuse me, can I help you?'" says Tony.

At this point, Tony did not think he was seeing a ghost. He assumed he was dealing with a living person, as he notes: "She looked totally solid. I thought it was somebody who had come in. I said, 'Can I help you?' And then she just looked at me like she was ignoring me, turned, and walked back into the front room. So I walked in to tell her, 'Hey, what are you doing in my house?' And there was nobody there."

Tony searched the entire house, but he was alone. He thought to himself, "Now that's kind of weird."

A few minutes later, his roommate, Mark, returned. Tony asked him, "Did you come in here a minute ago?" It was a stupid question, he knew — he had seen a Mexican woman, not a white man, but he was grasping for straws, searching for a logical explanation.

"No," Mark replied.

"Were you expecting someone to come over?" Tony asked.

"No," Mark asked. "Why?"

Tony decided to tell Mark what happened, adding, "You know what? I think this house is haunted."

"No, no, no," Mark shook his head. "Why?"

"I'm telling you," Tony said, "the last couple of days I've been catching movement out of the corner of my eye. And now... I thought it was my imagination, but I just saw this lady."

"You're kidding!" Mark said.

"No, I swear," Tony said.

Despite his assurances that he was telling the truth, though, Mark didn't believe him.

It wasn't long before Tony had a third encounter. About a week later, Tony was alone in the house in the kitchen when he again saw movement out of the corner of his eye. "I turn and I look and I see this lady standing in the front room. She's standing in our dining room, looking at me in the kitchen. She was looking right at me and I was looking at her," says Tony.

He recognized the lady instantly as the same person he had seen in the kitchen. This time, Tony decided he would try to just remain calm and observe the apparition instead of trying to confront it. "I just kind of stopped and looked at her — and she just stood there and stared at me for a second. Then she turned and walked into the front room. So I walked in and followed her...and she's gone. When I walked in, she was gone. So I thought, 'Okay, that's weird. Our house is haunted. That's cool, but I'm not telling anybody,'" says Tony.

It was just a week or two later that Tony began to notice another phenomenon. Objects around the house would go missing and then turn up in strange places. The first time it happened, Tony was missing his car keys. He looked for them everywhere and finally found them in the refrigerator. Soon, other similar incidents occurred. His wallet would suddenly be missing and he'd find it in the closet.

Usually, however, it was his car keys, which he kept finding in weird places all over the house, but usually in the refrigerator. Tony confronted Mark, who denied moving his keys.

Tony said, "Then this house is haunted."

"No, no, no," Mark shook his head.

Tony repeated, "No, this house is haunted."

Time went by and strange incidents continued to occur. At one point, Tony decided to trim the overgrown rose bushes. First he purchased and read a book on the subject. Then one morning he brought the tools out and began working on the garden. Shortly after he began, he set the pruning shears down, but when he bent down to pick them back up, they were gone. After searching for them for twenty minutes, he gave up and stopped trimming the bushes. Later on, he found the pruning shears in the closet.

On another occasion, the same thing happened. Tony went out to trim the rose bushes. Halfway through, the shears disappeared. When the same thing happened a third time, Tony recognized a pattern. "I would go out and start doing some gardening, and the gardening tools would disappear. If you set them down, they'd be gone, and you'd have to look around for them. You'd usually find them someplace in the house, or someplace weird, like how the hell did that get there?" says Tony.

Tony realized in hindsight that the lady ghost might have become annoyed that he was messing around in her garden. Even though the rose bushes began to bloom again, the gardening tools continued to be the target of activity.

Up to this point, Tony was the only one who had seen the ghost. His roommate Mark still remained skeptical. Then one day Tony's friend John (pseudonym) came over to visit. They were sitting on the couch talking when Tony realized that John was no longer looking at him, but instead was looking behind him into the hallway. Furthermore, John had an expression of surprise on his face — his eyes became large and he turned deathly pale.

"Are you alright?" Tony asked, concerned. John didn't answer, but continued staring.

"Are you alright?" Tony repeated. John stood up and Tony whirled around to see what John was looking at. Nothing was there.

"Did you see that!?" John asked. He ran over to the hallway. "Did you see that? Did you see it?"

"See what?"

John hesitated before blurting out, "Tony, there was a lady in your hallway! It was the weirdest thing!"

"What did you see?" Tony asked. "Because you look weird."

According to John, "While I was talking to you, I could see what looked like smoke coming into the hall, like mist. At first I didn't think it was anything, but as I was talking to you, then I thought maybe there was a fire in the kitchen because it was getting a little mistier. And as I was watching this mist, it started taking shape, and all of a sudden this lady was standing there."

Tony was amazed and asked John, "Was it an old lady?"

"Yes!" John replied. "Some little old lady."

Tony realized he had to tell John about his ghost. "I've seen her," he said. "I didn't want to tell you this, but I think my house is haunted."

"I know your house is haunted," John echoed. "I just saw it. That was the weirdest thing...that freaked me out."

Tony was glad that, finally, someone else had also seen the ghost. He wasn't crazy. His house was haunted. Still, he had no idea who the ghost was.

Then one day Tony's neighbor, Ruby, came over to visit. Without any prompting from Tony, Ruby began to talk about the former owners of the house. She said that an older couple lived there. First the husband died, and the wife lived there alone for several years.

Then one day she fell down in her bedroom. "You know," said Ruby, "she died in your bedroom."

Ruby explained that the old lady — whose name was Augustine — had fallen down and wasn't able to get up. When her grandson came to visit a week later, she had already died. She had been dead for several days before anybody noticed.

Ruby apologized and said, "I probably shouldn't have told you that because it makes some people kind of scared."

Tony shook his head. "Well, you know, that explains a lot because this house is haunted by her."

"You're kidding!" Ruby exclaimed.

"No," Tony said. "I've seen this old lady in the house a few times. A friend of mine saw her. There's somebody in this house."

"Wow, that's really interesting," Ruby said. "She really loved her house."

Now that Tony knew the identity of his ghost, he became even more intrigued by her presence. Whenever there was activity in the house, he would call her by name, saying, "Hey, Augustine, how are you doing?"

Interestingly, Tony noticed a corresponding increase in activity. More objects would be mysteriously moved or go missing. He started smelling the scent of lavender perfume floating around the house. Lights would be turned on when he was sure he had turned them off. A few times, he'd be watching television and it would suddenly turn off by itself, or it would turn on when he was in the other room.

Around this time, his old roommate, Mark, moved out and his new roommate, Rick (pseudonym), moved in. Tony told Rick about the ghost shortly after he moved in. To Tony's surprise, Rick admitted that he had already noticed that things were being moved around in the house.

For Tony, it was mostly his car keys. One time they turned up missing again. After a quick search, Tony realized it would take him twenty minutes to find the keys, which would end up being in some location where he would never put them. So this time, he talked out loud to the ghost, saying, "Augustine, I'm kind of in a hurry, could you please give me my keys back?"

Tony then looked around again and found the keys right by the front door. They had not been there a moment before. Tony says this is only one of several instances in which Augustine seemed to react to him and his roommate. Both he and Rick quickly learned to enjoy having Augustine around. They never feared her, and instead felt comforted by her presence. They even joked with her, trying to get her to clean up the kitchen dishes (which unfortunately she never did!)

For the next twelve years, Tony, Rick, and Augustine lived together peacefully. Augustine continued to perform her usual tricks: moving objects around, turning the television on and off, and hiding the gardening tools. Although it was much more rare, Tony and Rick would catch occasional glimpses of her.

"I'd be sitting around watching TV and I'd see her in the kitchen. I'd see her turn and look into the front room, and then turn and go back into the kitchen...I'd only see her in the house, and usually most of the time, it would be in the kitchen, or in the living room or dining room area that I'd see her. And she'd usually come in and she would look around," says Tony. "I think it was like she was just checking to see that things were the way she liked them. That's what I think the whole thing was — she wanted things the way she liked them."

Augustine became a member of the family and the three people — two living and one dead — lived together for many years. Then, after twelve years, the day came that Tony and Rick had to move out. They found a new place to live and were ready to move. After they had everything packed up and were doing their last walk-through of the house, the subject of Augustine finally came up.

"Well?" asked Rick.

Tony decided that they should at least say goodbye to her. Talking out loud to her, he said, "Hey, Augustine, we're moving. We've got a new place, and you're welcome to come with us if you want. It's been really nice living with you for the last twelve years. If you want, you can come with us to our new house."

Tony and Rick walked out of the house for the last time. Rick turned to Tony, "Do you think she'll come with us."

"No," Tony said. "I think she'll stay at her house. This is her house. This is where she likes it."

"It was kind of cool having her around," Rick sighed.

"Yeah," said Tony. "It was."

"I felt like I could leave the house unlocked, and she'd keep an eye on things."

"I know," Tony said. "Me too."

Tony and Rick never saw Augustine again. However, as far as they know, their disembodied roommate continues to haunt an innocent looking house in an affluent suburb of Inglewood.

But First There Was Harry...

While Tony never did see the ghost of Augustine again, he reports that he has had a long history of seeing ghosts. He had ghost encounters as kid and he has also seen ghosts following his encounters with the spirit of Augustine.

Tony's first experience with ghosts began in his pre-teen years and involved a poltergeist that was somehow attached to him.

"I used to have an imaginary friend when I was a kid that used to do things, like a poltergeist," says Tony, "but I think there was something more tangible to it than just an imaginary friend or something imaginary because I could get it to do things."

Tony called his imaginary friend/poltergeist "Harry." At first he assumed that Harry was imaginary, but then strange things began to happen. He would wish for something to happen or actually ask Harry to make something happen, and then it would. More often than not, Harry seemed to act of his own accord, but in a way that Tony would always appear to be responsible for the event. Tony's only explanation for how something like this could happen was that Harry must be responsible. If Tony got angry, Harry would sometimes become active, throwing various objects across the room.

"*It* used to tease my younger brother. *It* would throw things at him and he would blame me for it," says Tony.

One evening, Tony was lying in bed and his brother was also in bed. At the time they shared a room. Suddenly his brother said, "Are you throwing something at me?"

"No," Tony replied.

"Who threw the socks then?" His brother held up a bundled pair of socks.

"I didn't throw the socks," Tony protested. "I'm right here."

"Well somebody threw them!" his brother said.

Tony knew it wasn't him, and obviously his brother didn't throw the socks at himself. It could only be Tony's poltergeist friend. Knowing what the reaction would be, he said, "I think it's Harry."

His brother groaned. Tony had long ago learned that his family didn't believe in Harry and they were tired of his insistence that Harry was responsible for various events. "Not that stupid Harry!" his brother barked. "Don't talk about him!"

Tony shrugged and turned to go back to sleep. This was typical of how Harry got him into trouble. Nobody believed him and, yet, Tony knew he was not responsible for all the mischief he was being accused of — at least not physically responsible. To him, the explanation was simple — it was Harry.

"Everybody in my family said don't talk about him. I would say, 'I'm telling you guys, you're going to get him mad, and he's going to go break a dish or something.' And sometimes...something would fall off the counter or the shelves. My mom's vase would fall off and break. And I used to try and experiment with it," says Tony.

Tony says that while Harry was active during his pre-teen and early teenage years, the activity eventually slowed down and then pretty much stopped entirely. He later did some experimenting with the Ouija board and then moved into the haunted house in Inglewood where he had numerous encounters with the ghost of Augustine.

Ghost in the Mirror....

Following this, he soon had another dramatic series of encounters with a ghost, in this case involving the spirit of his recently deceased older brother, Leonard. Interestingly, most of these encounters involved an apparition that could only be seen in the reflection of a certain mirror.

Part of the wall to the den in the house was covered with a large mirrored surface. As the television was located in the den, Tony spent many hours sitting on the couch watching TV. In this position, Tony was facing the mirrored wall, which reflected back into the kitchen area. It was here that Tony had many encounters with the ghost of his brother, Leonard.

Tony's brother died while he was still only middle-aged, so it was a tragic loss for the family, and especially for Tony who was very close to him. In fact, Leonard had recently moved in with Tony and lived with him for a period of time. However, it wasn't long after Leonard's death that Tony began seeing his apparition.

"I would see him every so often. I'd be sitting in the den, and I'd see him come into the kitchen. I'd see him in the mirror. Every so often, I'd be sitting there watching TV, and in the mirror, I could see him in the kitchen. I could see him sometimes standing there. Or he'd be walking into the kitchen."

The first few times this happened, Tony whirled around and looked behind him...only to see that the kitchen was empty. However, he eventually learned that he would see more if he remained looking at the mirror.

In the first few years following Leonard's death, Tony had several of these kinds of encounters. In almost all of them, there was no real interaction between the brothers. Leonard did seem to be aware of his surroundings, but he also didn't appear to try and communicate with Tony.

However, according to Tony, there were a few occasions during which there was a definite communication between them. "I would see him standing there in the kitchen and I would see him looking at me in the mirror...and I would just say, 'Hey, Leonard.' And then he'd walk away and be gone."

Tony's encounters with the spirit of his brother Leonard were not exclusively confined to reflections in the mirror. There were several occasions where he was walking by the kitchen when he caught sight of Leonard's apparition out of the corner of his eye. However, he never saw him close-up or face-to-face. Tony never doubted that his mirror encounters with Leonard were anything but totally real. He had already had so many experiences with ghosts that he was, of course, totally convinced of their reality. However, he does admit that he did enjoy receiving confirmation of the haunting from an independent witness.

At the time, Tony had invited a roommate to share the house with him. The roommate was a friend of his named Sarah (pseudonym). Tony didn't tell Sarah about Leonard because he didn't think that Leonard would try to appear to her. He was also confident that Leonard would never purposefully scare anyone.

Then one weekend, Tony decided to go camping, leaving Sarah alone in the house. When Tony returned a few days later, Sarah rushed up to him and said, "I think this house is haunted, Tony."

Sarah had no idea that there was any paranormal activity going on in the house. She was sitting on the couch in the front room when it happened. Says Sarah:

"I saw this guy come walking into the front room. I thought he came in through the front door. I looked up and I saw him standing there, and he just kind of looked at me and smiled. And I went, 'Uh, can I help you?' And he turned and walked into the kitchen. I got up and said, 'Hey, Tony's not here. Are you looking for Tony?' And I got up and I looked, and there was nobody there. I looked all around because it freaked me out. I thought maybe they were hiding or something."

As Sarah gushed out her story, Tony could see that she was a little shaken up. "I think this house is haunted," she repeated.

"It probably is," Tony told her, "but it's a good thing."

"What do you mean?" Sarah asked.

Before he answered, Tony decided to make sure that the figure Sarah had seen was, in fact, Leonard. "Well, what did he look like?" he asked.

"Well, I've never seen him before," she replied, "He was kind of tall and thin."

"Dark hair?" Tony asked.

"Yeah!" Sarah said, surprised.

Tony whipped out a picture of his brother and showed it to her. "Did he look like this?" he asked.

"That's him!" Sarah screamed.

"This is my older brother," Tony told her. "He's passed away."

"I think this house is haunted," she repeated.

Tony echoed her, "It probably is, but at least it's a good thing."

Eventually Leonard's ghost stopped appearing. Since then, Tony has had no further encounters. However, with his track record, it probably won't be too long before he has another encounter with ghosts.

Chapter Eight

A Ouija Board Nightmare

In most cases, encountering a ghost appears to be a random event. Paranormal manifestations are difficult to predict, and therefore, difficult to study. However, there are some cases in which ghosts can be provoked into appearing. Sometimes simply speaking to a ghost, asking for a sign, or for them to do something specific can cause a reaction. Sometimes, hauntings become activated when somebody angers the ghost, perhaps by remodeling their home or performing some other action that threatens the ghost's sense of privacy or personal space.

Perhaps the most common method that can provoke a ghost into appearing is a popular game known as the Ouija Board. While this game is sold in toy stores, it has actually been practiced for thousands of years. A ouija board is nothing more than a board with letters and numbers painted on it. In and of itself, it has no special properties. However, it can be used as an effective tool to actually initiate an encounter with a ghost.

The process is simple, though the mechanics are not well understood. It involves one or more people sitting around the board and placing their fingers on the pointer, which spells out messages on the board allegedly from the deceased. However, what is causing the pointer to move remains controversial. Ghost researchers say that spirit energy is involved while skeptics say that the participants are moving the pointer either consciously or unconsciously.

The following cases appear to validate the first explanation. In the next two cases, people began using the Ouija board an in attempt to contact spirits. In both cases, they were apparently successful. However, in both cases, they also learned to regret their decision to open their homes to ghosts.

"Eye" of the Storm in San Fernando

The first case involves a group of siblings who, as children in their home in San Fernando on the eastern edge of the San Fernando Valley, obtained a Ouija board and began using it on a regular basis.

David Fleetwood was about eight years old when he first tried it with his older brother and sisters and their friends. They all sat down in one of their bedrooms, pulled out the board, and sat in a circle around it. This particular Ouija board had a pointer that was shaped like an eye. It was a wooden frame with a hollow center. When the eye moved across the board, it would stop over a letter, which would appear in the center of the eye.

David's siblings had already used the board many times. When David placed his fingers on the eye along with the others, he was amazed by the way it would move — *seemingly by itself* — spelling out various messages.

"We were calling ghosts. They would get certain spirits every so often," says David. "I used to wonder about it...whether or not they were actually moving it or not."

David and his siblings used the board many times after that, calling on various spirits and trying to get interesting messages. What interested David the most, however, was not the information coming from the board, but rather the way the eye seemed to move by itself.

"We would really get it going for real, because it would get to the point where our fingertips wouldn't even be touching it, and it would wiggle and move. It was kind of unexplained," says David.

David, though, found the experience a little creepy and he eventually stopped "playing" with the board. After awhile, most of his siblings and friends also became bored with it and found other ways to entertain themselves. All except for his older sister, Elizabeth, and her friend Belinda (pseudonyms). Ever since she was a young girl, Elizabeth was interested in the supernatural. As a teenager, she read several books about various paranormal subjects and held numerous séances and sessions with the Ouija board.

Like David, Elizabeth remembers using the Ouija board to contact various spirits. She also remembers how the eye would move by itself. On a few occasions, she experienced supernatural events that seemed to be connected to her séances. One of the most dramatic was the time a black crow appeared in her bedroom closet during a séance. They heard something flapping around inside, opened the closet, and the bird began flying around the room.

On another occasion, Elizabeth and Belinda were in Elizabeth's bedroom playing with the Ouija board. David remembers this particular incident as if it happened yesterday. He was twelve years old and wanted to stay and watch. His sister didn't appreciate the interference of her younger brother, but told him that he could watch them from the hallway.

David was satisfied with this and, standing in the doorway, he watched his sister and her friend sit down on the bed and begin using the Ouija board. As usual, they sat across from each other, placed their fingers lightly on the eye, and began talking out loud to the spirits, asking various questions. Everything seemed to be going normal when, suddenly, something happened that had never happened before. Says David:

"The eye — the pointer — it was moving, then all of a sudden, the pointer on the board started levitating. I'm not talking about it levitating an inch or two. It levitated high enough to where both girls took their hands off the eye. The pointer...the thing continued to levitate up towards their faces. It levitated up maybe two feet and then kind of jolted towards my sister Elizabeth and hit her in the neck-chest area and just fell down."

At this moment, all three children screamed in terror and went running out of the room. David remembers being "freaked out," though Elizabeth was less so and Belinda didn't seem perturbed much at all. Elizabeth wasn't hurt by the pointer, only startled. However, more than an hour passed before the three of them ventured back into the bedroom to look at the board and discuss what happened.

It was then that Belinda revealed that she was very familiar with ghosts and the ouija board because her mom claimed to be

"Then, all of a sudden, the pointer on the board started levitating. I'm not talking about it levitating an inch or two — it levitated high enough to where both girls took their hands off the pointer, and it continued to levitate up towards their faces."

a "black witch." Belinda explained that she lived with her father, but that she had been around her mother enough to learn that the supernatural is, in fact, very real. That was why, she said, she wasn't particularly frightened by what had happened. She had already seen much worse.

David, however, remembers the event as one of the strangest incidents in his life. As he says, "I was standing at the doorway, four feet away. When the thing rose up, they both jumped back, and the thing was still there...rising up...and then it lurched towards her... I got a little spooked over that. I'll never forget that day. You don't forget stuff like that. Playing with trucks and army men comes and goes. Something levitating — and you're twelve years old — that sticks with you."

Since then, David has never used the Ouija board again. While his sister continues to maintain a strong interest in the paranormal, David remains a little wary. He still finds it interesting, however, he is hesitant to use the board again or attend any type of séance. Recently he had an opportunity to visit a well-known medium and, while intrigued, he wasn't quite ready to attend. However, he does admit that he is a believer in ghosts, but he warns that the Ouija board is more than just an innocent little children's game.

Intrigued with Spirits

The second case of Ouija board regret involves Tony Tocco. As a young man, Tony was intrigued with the idea of contacting spirits and purchased a Ouija board. At the time he was renting a room with his girlfriend, Jenna (pseudonym). It was a garage converted into a studio apartment in Gardena, on the south side of the Greater Los Angeles area.

One evening they were looking for something to do. They decided to bring out the Ouija board to see if they could contact a spirit from "the other side."

They pulled out the board, placed it between them, and put their fingers lightly on the pointer. Tony then spoke out loud, asking if there were any spirits out there who would like to communicate with them. To their shock, the pointer began to move.

It didn't happen immediately. In fact, for the first few minutes the pointer remained motionless. Then, just when they were beginning to wonder if it would work, it began to spell out intelligible messages. Tony and Jenna asked the spirit for a name, and the spirit quickly identified itself as "Joe."

This began the first of what would become a series of communications with "Joe." The first time they contacted Joe, the pointer moved slowly and haltingly, and they were only able to get a few messages. However, intrigued by their success, Tony and Jenna decided to try again.

A few nights later, they pulled out the board again. About a minute after they put their fingers on the pointer, it began to move, again spelling out the name Joe. They asked questions, and Joe slowly answered. This time, the pointer seemed to move more easily and purposefully. Tony wondered if Jenna was playing with him and moving the pointer herself. Meanwhile, Jenna wondered the same thing. However, neither was ready to accuse the other of hoaxing and continued their "playing."

For the next few weeks, they played with the board on an almost nightly basis. Each time, Joe popped up and began to answer their questions. After several more times, the pointer moved with astonishing swiftness and accuracy. In fact, every time they played, Joe seemed to get better and better at maneuvering the pointer.

"It was a trip," said Tony. "I noticed that the more we played with it, the faster it would respond and be more active...The first few times we did it, we'd have to sit there and wait for it to move. After about four or five days of playing with it every night, as soon as we'd sit down and put our fingers on it, it would start moving and then we'd get this Joe. It wasn't anybody we tried to contact. It was just this one person who kept coming up...he was the one who started telling us things."

At first, the messages that came from the board and Joe were innocuous and unmemorable, but as time went on, the messages became more meaningful. Before long, the board actually started to accurately predict future events. Most of the predictions were little things — an upcoming visit from a friend, a phone call, and other possibly coincidental things. However, both Tony and Jenna were intrigued by the information and decided to continue.

When the accuracy of the messages increased, Tony again began to wonder if Jenna was moving the pointer herself. Meanwhile, Jenna was still suspicious that Tony was the one pulling a hoax and that he was actually moving it himself. Coincidentally, each of them decided to test their theory at the same moment...during the same Ouija board session.

As usual, they sat sitting down with the board between them, called forth Joe, and began asking him questions. On this occasion, the pointer was moving incredibly fast. Whatever force was allegedly moving the pointer, it seemed to be more powerful than the times before.

They asked Joe another question and the pointer began to dart strongly back and forth across the board. It was just about to finish spelling out a word when Tony decided it was time to see if Jenna was hoaxing him. He quickly pulled his hands off the pointer.

Meanwhile, Jenna also noticed that the pointer seemed to be moving more quickly than usual and thought that Tony was responsible, and so at the same exact moment that Tony pulled his hands off the pointer, so did she. To their shock, the pointer continued to move by itself, although neither of them was touching it.

Says Tony, "We both thought the same thing — of catching each other moving it — and we both pulled our hands off. And it ended up finishing the word. It had about three more letters. It spelled it out and finished it, and then it stopped."

At this point, Jenna looked over at Tony in fear and surprise. "You weren't moving it!"

"No," Tony whispered. "You weren't moving it either," he said rhetorically.

"Whoa! That's weird," Jenna said, pushing away from the board. "This is freaky. This is too weird. I'm not playing with this anymore."

"What?" Tony said. "Now we've really got to see because that thing moved by itself! We've got to see what's going on!"

"No, Tony," his girlfriend shook her head. "That was scary. This is too scary. I'm not playing with it anymore."

At Jenna's insistence, Tony put the board away for the night. However, a few nights later, he brought out the board again. Somehow, he convinced Jenna to give it another try. She refused at first, but Tony kept asking, and she finally relented. They began to use the board again on a regular basis, talking with Joe and trying to get some useful information.

Again, the messages that came through the board were sometimes surprisingly accurate, but then an incident occurred that put a sudden and complete halt to their investigations.

"Joe kept coming to the Ouija board. Every time we would get together, it would come out and talk to us... It told us things, and then the things happened, and we were like, 'hmmm...it told us about her grandmother, that her grandmother was going to get hurt, and she did,'" says Tony. "Some of them, we'd never get a chance to verify if what it said was real or not, but after this ghost told us that her grandmother was going to have a fall and get injured, and she did — about two days later she fell and broke her arm — it was like, 'Whoa! This is kind of creepy.'"

While Joe and his accurate predictions intrigued Tony, this last incident badly frightened Jenna. She refused to play with board ever again. The next time Tony brought it out, Jenna said, "I'm not doing it with you now, Tony. It's too scary."

"Why?" Tony asked. "Now this is getting interesting. Now we know there's something going on with this thing, and we've got to figure it out."

"No," Jenna said. "It's too scary because now there's really somebody out there. I'm not doing this."

Tony could see that it was useless to argue. Jenna was done with the Ouija board and absolutely would not play with it. Not wanting to upset her, and also realizing that he might be playing with forces beyond his control, Tony agreed to not use the board anymore. They both learned the hard way that it's not always a good idea to play around with ghosts.

Chapter Nine

A Native American Haunting

Hundreds of years ago, the Greater Los Angeles area was populated by several Native American tribes, including the Chumash and the Gabrielanos. However, the march of time brought a steady stream of settlers from Mexico and the eastern United States. The Native American population was eventually almost entirely displaced.

Not surprisingly, this did not occur without conflict and tragedy. As a result, there are now several locations throughout the Greater Los Angeles area that are known to contain Native American ghosts. One such place is Topanga Canyon State Park. Numerous reports of Native American ghosts have come from this area. Much of the activity has occurred where homes were allegedly built over a Native American Burial Ground. Another location is the intersection of Hollywood Boulevard and Sierra Bonita in the city of Hollywood. In this area, numerous witnesses have heard the sounds of Native American music and seen full-color apparitions.

Yet another area that has earned a reputation among the locals for Native American ghosts is Mount Washington, located in Glendale off State Highway 2, on the eastern edge of Los Angeles County. Back in the early 1800s, a tribe of Native Americans lived at the eastern-facing base of Mount Washington, but, at some point, the entire tribe was wiped out by a large group of marauders and bandits.

Today the area is a large housing tract. At the base of the mountain where the alleged tragedy actually took place, there is a large cement gully that was constructed by the State to control the flood runoff from the mountain, where there used to be a natural river. The area is cordoned off by a chain-link fence to prevent anybody from falling into the wash.

The first indication that something strange was going on in the area was when a group of children were playing alongside the fence that overlooks the wash. They *all saw* another group of children playing on the other side of the fence — inside the wash where the water was. The children had, of course, been forbidden by their parents from climbing the fence and going into the wash, so when they saw this other group of children, they all became jealous.

They became even more envious when they saw that the other children were not only allowed to play in the river, they were all dressed up in really elaborate and authentic-looking Indian costumes, complete with leather pants, skirts, vests, and headbands. Their clothes were also decorated with colorful beads and bird-feathers.

The group of Native American children seemed to pay no attention to the other children, but continued to play in the water of the wash. Seeing this, the other children ran home to tell their parents and ask if they could get an Indian costume and play with the other children.

Melissa Jarvis (not her real name), who lived in the area, says her son came home and asked her if he could dress up like an Indian like the other kids in the neighborhood.

Melissa asked her son where he had seen these other kids. He explained that there was a group of them playing in the wash. He said that they were all children around his age and were dressed up just like real Indians.

Melissa told him that those kids should not be playing in the wash, that it was dangerous, and their parents should be alerted to this fact. Later, she asked around the neighborhood and found that other children in the area had also seen the children in the wash dressed up as Indians, but nobody seemed to know whom their parents were. However, she did learn that several of the children had also asked their parents if they could also dress up like Indians and go play in the wash.

A short time later, it happened again. Her son came running home and said that the Indian children were out there playing in the wash again. This time, Melissa asked her son to take her outside and show her. Her son led her to the area and pointed to the children. "There they are," he said.

"Where?" Melissa asked, looking over what appeared to be an empty wash.

"Well, mom, they're right over there!" he said, pointing.

Melissa couldn't see anything. Her son kept insisting, however, that they were right there. Whatever her son was looking at, clearly only he could see it. Or them? It was at this point that Melissa wondered if they might be dealing with ghosts.

After they returned inside, she asked her son to describe the children again. Her son explained that they had leather clothes on, with beads and feathers, and that their skin was dark.

That evening, after Melissa told her husband what had happened, they decided to do some research. To their surprise, they discovered that a small tribe of Native Americans did live in the area, but in the early 1800s, and they had been ruthlessly killed by bandits. Unfortunately, the tragedy appears to have resulted in a haunting...one that is still going on today.

"There was a group of them playing in the wash. He said that they were all children around his age and were dressed up just like real Indians... Melissa couldn't see anything. Her son kept insisting, however, that they were right there."

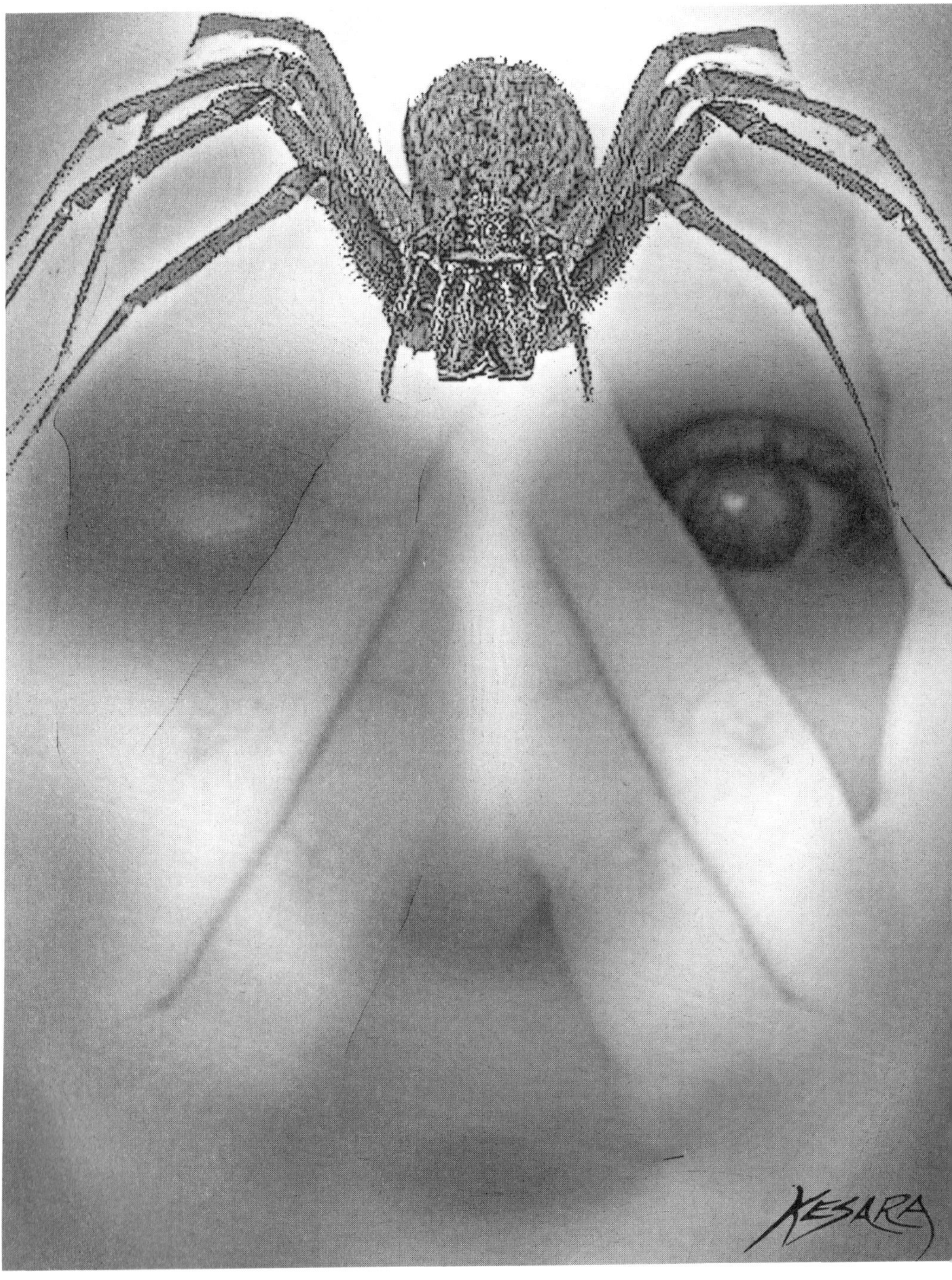

"There is a spirit in this house. There is a spirit. I can feel it. The spirit is trying to tell Samantha something. It's trying to show her something. It scared her."

Chapter Ten

A Haunting in Pacoima

In the late 1950s, Connie Lopez and her family moved into a small home in the suburbs of Pacoima. The home had been previously occupied by one other family, but otherwise, was practically new. It was a three-bedroom home. Connie and her husband, of course, slept in the master bedroom. Their infant son had his own bedroom and their two daughters shared the third.

When they moved in, their youngest daughter Samantha (not her real name) was only three-years-old. One evening after dinner, Samantha was playing alone in her bedroom. Realizing that she hadn't heard her for a while, Connie walked into the room to check-up on her daughter. To her concern, little Samantha, who was normally a very happy and carefree child, was sitting in a corner all by herself. She had a scared expression, and looked to Connie like she had seen some type of ghost.

"I went to pick her up and she started screaming, and I mean SCREAMING like I've never heard her scream. I never had experienced anything like that with her. I kept asking her, 'Samantha, what's wrong?! Samantha, what's wrong?!' And she didn't say anything for a while. She just lied down. So I thought, 'Oh, my God, maybe she's getting sick. Maybe she ate something.' I didn't know what to think," says Connie.

Connie held Samantha, then gave her a bath, and tucked her into her bed. She turned out the lights and put on the nightlight and walked out of the room. At that moment, Samantha started screaming again.

This time, both Connie and her husband ran back into the bedroom to comfort not only her, but also their other five-year-old daughter who was becoming scared by Samantha's outbursts.

"We didn't know what to do," says Connie. "We thought maybe something happened to her. We checked her. I asked her, 'Samantha, what's wrong?' But she just cried, and I mean, crying. We had to get my other daughter out of there because it was scaring the daylights out of her.

"I kept saying, 'Samantha, what's wrong? Samantha?' She couldn't talk. She couldn't say anything."

Eventually Samantha fell asleep. However, the next night, it was a repeat performance. As soon as they put her to bed, she would start screaming at the top of her lungs — and she wouldn't stop until she fell asleep.

The third night brought the same thing. By this time, Connie and her husband were extremely concerned for their daughter. They sent their other children to live with their aunt so they could give Samantha their full attention.

Still, Samantha's episodes continued. It seemed to Connie that her daughter had been terribly traumatized by something, but Samantha refused to talk about what had happened. Still, Connie persisted in questioning her, and finally, her persistence paid off and Samantha began to talk.

Says Connie, "All she ever did was cry, cry, cry. I said, 'Samantha, what is wrong? Where does it hurt?' I grabbed her and I held her and hugged her and said, 'Samantha, tell me where it hurts. Tell me. Something is wrong. What is it?' She just shook her head, saying nothing.

"And then all of a sudden she stopped crying. And then she put her hands over my face and said, 'Don't move, mom! Don't move!'"

Connie looked at her frightened daughter and said, "Why?"

Samantha replied, "There's a big spider right on your face!" Then Samantha screamed that there were spiders all over, and she jumped off of her mother and ran to the corner of the bedroom.

This behavior continued for the next month. Each time it happened, Connie would tell her, "Samantha, there are no spiders!"

Samantha, however, would insist, "Yes, momma, yes! Don't move because he's coming. He's climbing over you! He's all over your face, your hair, your clothes!"

"Samantha," Connie insisted, "There's nothing."

By this time, Connie and her husband were concerned that their daughter was having some severe mental problems. Samantha's condition was causing all of them to lose sleep. It was time to take her to see the doctor.

When Connie and her husband brought Samantha in, the doctor asked Connie to explain what was wrong. Connie did so, and then the doctor conducted a brief examination of Samantha.

The doctor then turned to Connie and said that he believed he knew what was wrong. He told Connie, "It's because you have a new baby. She's probably feeling spoiled and needs attention, and this is what she's doing. She's feeling neglected. There's a reason she's doing all this. It's only for attention."

Connie protested and disagreed. She told the doctor that this was not normal behavior for Samantha, and that Samantha was not only hysterical, she was seeing things. Away from the house, her daughter seemed to be fine. Her episodes appeared to occur exclusively at home.

The doctor said, "The next time she does that, you need to put her in the room, close the door, and hold the door closed so she doesn't get out. Let her have her tantrum."

This upset Connie even further, and she insisted that the doctor give Samantha a complete physical examination. The doctor reluctantly agreed and said to bring her back for some tests. They returned that week for a full examination. The doctor could find nothing wrong.

Wondering if the doctor might be right, Connie tried spoiling Samantha with her love and attention. Nothing, however, seemed to get through to her daughter.

"She wouldn't move. She wouldn't talk. She wouldn't do anything," says Connie. "We tried to talk to her. We tried to take her shopping, buy whatever she wanted. She didn't want anything. She only wanted to be out of the house. She wanted to be out of the house."

Connie decided that she would start sleeping with Samantha in Samantha's bedroom. As soon as Connie would turn out the lights, however, Samantha would say, "Don't turn out the lights."

Connie would turn them on and say, "Okay, but we need to get some sleep. You need to get some sleep, Samantha, because you're tired."

Samantha, however, refused to sleep. After a full month of this, Connie had reached her breaking point. "She wouldn't even close her eyes. She lay there with her eyes open," says Connie, "and then she started crying hysterically again because there were more bugs on my face, more spiders. And that was it. I lost it, and I started crying."

Connie and her husband discussed Samantha's condition for the hundredth time. "What is wrong with her?" the husband asked Connie.

"I don't know," Connie replied. "I don't know what to do. I don't know what to tell her."

Connie called her aunt and told her about the latest developments. Finally her aunt said that she might have a solution. Since the conventional doctors hadn't been able to solve Samantha's problem or give a diagnosis, her aunt thought another approach might be more effective.

"We're going to take her to a lady," Connie's aunt said. "I know a lady. A healer."

Connie's aunt had arthritis in her legs, and she sometimes found relief through the administrations of a local psychic healer. Connie and her husband were at the end of their rope. They speculated that Samantha's condition might be spiritual, so perhaps a visit to the psychic healer would help. Certainly it couldn't hurt.

Connie had never been to a healer, so she had no idea what to expect. She arrived, and the healer instructed her to lay Samantha on a small table. The healer then took out a carton of a dozen eggs. She held each one under a bright light and asked Connie to verify that these were all real eggs.

Connie examined the eggs, each of which appeared to be a normal fresh egg. The eggs were then set to the side while the healer grabbed a bouquet of flowers.

The healer took the flowers and began to pray intently. She then took the flowers and began to pass them back and forth over Samantha's body in wide sweeping passes, brushing her body gently with the bouquet.

Connie could hardly believe what happened next. She says, "The flowers, right in front of my face, started drying and dried up totally. They totally dried up."

The healer then picked up an egg and cracked it, showing Connie that the eggs were fresh. She then held up another egg, handed it to Connie, and asked her to verify that it was a real egg. Connie held the egg, which felt cool in her hand. The healer then took the egg back and began passing it back and forth over Samantha's body. Samantha remained perfectly still during the entire procedure.

Curious, Connie kept her eyes riveted on the egg. Says Connie, "This egg, all of a sudden, it just got dark. And she cracked it open and the egg was black. The egg was literally black. And she said, there is something in your house. Some spirit has come to Samantha and scared her. If you don't do something, Samantha is going to have a nervous breakdown."

Armed with this information, Connie and her husband decided that perhaps Samantha's condition would improve if they moved her out of the house. They took her over to their aunt's and picked up the other two children and took them home.

Samantha's condition immediately began to improve. They tried to take her back home for an evening, but Samantha immediately began screaming. Connie reluctantly returned Samantha to her aunt's house.

While Samantha seemed to be doing better away from the house, there was clearly still a problem that needed to be solved. Samantha couldn't live with her aunt forever. They decided to bring in a priest. The priest agreed to walk through the house, blessing each room as he went.

Meanwhile, the psychic healer asked Connie if she could come to the house and try to communicate with the spirit that she believed was haunting her daughter's bedroom.

Connie agreed and took the healer into her daughter's bedroom. What the healer said next gave Connie little comfort. The healer walked through the room and said, "Connie, there is a spirit in this house. There is a spirit. I can feel it. The spirit is trying to tell Samantha something. It's trying to show her something. It scared her."

That was enough for Connie and her husband. They decided to just sell the house and move. They immediately began packing and, two days later, they moved out. They found a new house within a week and moved in. Samantha was put in her new bedroom and slept normally for the first time in months.

"It was like nothing ever happened," says Connie. "As a matter of fact, she never remembered it. From the time we left, she never remembered what happened to her...It was so strange, because from the time we took her out of the house, it was like her whole life just opened up. She smiled. She talked. She walked around. She played outside."

Meanwhile, the psychic healer did some research on Connie's former house and discovered that somebody had died in the house. A member of the family of the previous owners died in the house, though the healer was not able to determine the exact identity.

A new family moved into the house. Later, Connie was talking to her former next-door neighbors, and discovered that the new family had found a large cache of money that had been hidden underneath the house. Connie now wonders if that's why the ghost appeared to Samantha and if he had been trying to communicate that with her.

Whatever the case, Connie believes that her three-year-old daughter had a terrifying encounter with a ghost from which she was only able to recover by leaving the area. Samantha, who is now grown-up and still has no memory of the incident, has reported no further encounters with ghosts.

Chapter Eleven

A Biting Ghost

Ghosts can manifest in a wide variety of ways. Most often, manifestations include apparitions, footsteps, cold spots, odors, self-moving objects, lights going on and off, doors opening and closing, mysterious exploding/crashing sounds, banging noises, sensing a presence...the list goes on and on. Each of these manifestations appears to be an attempt on the part of ghosts to make their selves known. In other words, many ghosts are trying to be noticed. They perform these behaviors because they want people to know that they are there. They are doing their best to communicate and pierce the veil that divides the physical dimension and the spiritual dimension.

While ghosts can apparently see the physical world, it is much more difficult for them to interact with it. The veil between this dimension and the next may be thin, but it is not always easily penetrated. The evidence collected by paranormal researchers shows that most ghosts are apparently unable to manipulate physical objects, so apparently it is a big deal for ghosts to affect the environment in any way.

Many hauntings are limited to only a few types of manifestations. Others hauntings, however, are much more active. In some of these cases, the ghosts have apparently learned how to manipulate their energies to make their selves known in a wide variety of ways. In a few cases, ghosts can become very aggressive, even to the extent of actually attacking a witness.

One such active haunting recently took place in Moorpark, where John Stone and his family moved into their new home in the early 1990s. The house had been previously occupied by another family, but otherwise, was in excellent condition.

"At first it started with kind of whispering voices, and sometimes I would hear my name called when nobody would be in the house… Some pretty strange stuff was going on."

It wasn't long after they moved in, however, that John and his family began to experience odd events. For John, it began with hearing strange noises. "At first it started with kind of whispering voices — and sometimes I would hear my name called when no one would be in the house," he says.

The first few times this occurred, John simply ignored it and didn't think anything of it. However, after he heard the voices on several different occasions, it became clear that, as John says, "some pretty strange stuff was going on."

One day he mentioned his experiences to his younger brother. That's when his brother revealed that he had also had some strange experiences in the house, including a face-to-face encounter with an actual apparition. According to John, "My brother told me that he saw a white apparition just move from one room into the other, through the hallway, going really fast."

Soon the ghost began to manifest in a wide variety of ways, including turning lights on and off, moving objects, opening and closing doors, and of course, more weird noises. Then came a manifestation that was so bizarre, John hesitated to reveal it to anyone. The ghost began to physically *bite* him.

Strangely, John was almost always asleep when it happened. "I would wake up in the middle of the night with bruises and teeth marks on my arms and legs," he says.

Unknown to John, this manifestation — while rare — is not unique. It has actually been reported in many other similar cases. Most often, this manifestation occurs in poltergeist-type hauntings. Whatever the case, the mysterious wounds appeared several times on John's body. They never caused him much pain and healed very quickly. Despite the alarming nature of the manifestations, it happened often enough that John was able to overcome his fear of the experience.

"At first it was a little bit unnerving," he says, "but after awhile, it really wasn't too bad because I wasn't getting hurt or anything."

Meanwhile, the ghost continued to manifest in other ways.

"My other brother, my older brother — he said he and his friends spent the night there and they heard doors opening and closing by themselves when everyone was asleep," says John.

While the haunting at John's home continued to occur, he also began having similar problems at his place of employment. John worked as a janitor at a theater called "The Moorpark Melodrama." It was not a movie theater, but a stage theater where people performed plays.

John's job entailed staying at the building late at night when nobody else was there, cleaning up, and closing the establishment. Shortly after he started, some of his fellow employees came up to him and warned him that there were ghosts in the building. Several actors told him that they had experienced their own encounters, including everything from ghostly footsteps and voices to full-color apparitions. The actors told John to be on the lookout for ghosts because, more than likely, he would see them too.

John soon had reason to believe them.

"After I began working there, I started having some of my own experiences. There was one night when I was cleaning up the aisles. I walked up, looked up at the projection booth, and I saw the face of someone kind of staring down. It didn't look like there was a body. It was just kind of a translucent face up in the window."

It wasn't long before John started having other strange experiences. Soon he almost became used to it. "There were other times I would be the only one in the building, cleaning up late at night, and after everything was done, I'd hear footsteps upstairs. I'd hear voices and stuff."

John no longer works at the Moorpark Melodrama, but he — like many of the other people who have worked there — is convinced that it is haunted.

Back at his home, the haunting did eventually quiet down.

"The activity has seemed to stop in the last couple of years... Every now and then something happens," says John, "but all the heavy activity seemed to be going on between 1992 and 1998. It happens sometimes here and there. I was sitting in my bed one night a couple of months ago, and I had a little bottle of Tylenol PM just fly straight off the nightstand and onto my bed. I was looking right at it. I happened to glance right over and saw it just kind of jump off and land on the bed. That's the last thing that happened. That one kind of scared me."

On a couple of occasions, John has taken photographs of his home in which strange orbs of light appear. They are not visible to the naked eye, but show up clearly in the photographs. Orbs are well-known in the paranormal community; many researchers believe orbs are spirits whose energy is invisible to our eyes, but which can be captured on film.

John has not been able to find out why his house is haunted, though he does have some theories.

"I haven't been able to find out if anyone died in the house... but I know that a lot of houses in this area where I live are built on sacred Indian burial grounds. That probably might have something to do with it," says John.

"The mirror...it really set my teeth on edge. It was beautiful, the frame was gorgeous, but I didn't want to get near it. It was like the mirror was throwing this negative energy at you. It was like some sort of portal..."

Chapter Twelve

A Haunted Bookshop

A location can become haunted for many different reasons. Some places are haunted because they are the location of a tragic death, such as a murder or fatal accident. Other locations are haunted by former long-dead residents, owners, and employees who have remained attached to their homes or places of business. Some hauntings, though, center on a person rather than a location. Then there are hauntings caused by objects.

This last category is perhaps one of the more rare causes of a haunting. In these types of cases, spirits seem to be attached to a physical possession. In this next case, a small bookshop called the Psychedelic Moon, located on Melrose Avenue in West Hollywood, became haunted because of the presence of two apparently haunted objects. One was a large mirror; the other was a book.

The bookshop specialized in an eclectic mixture of occult books, tie-dyed t-shirts, beads, black lights, lava lamps, and other items associated with the fringe hippy culture of the late 1960s and early 1970s.

An older couple named Gary and Linda (pseudonyms) owned and ran the bookshop. Much of their business involved rare and hard-to-find books, specializing in various aspects of the supernatural. So throughout the years, they had heard many stories from their customers about ghosts and other strange happenings, and had learned a little bit about the paranormal. However, it wasn't until they received a special request from one particular customer that they experienced their own foray into the unknown.

The customer was a self-proclaimed witch. She came into the bookshop one day and asked the owners if they were able to locate a number of hard-to-find books for her. Because that was their specialty, the owners took down the names of the titles and told the customer that they would attempt to get the books for her, and that they would call her when they arrived or if they weren't able to locate any copies. The woman agreed and left the bookshop. To their delight, they were able to locate the books without too much trouble and had them shipped to their shop. Almost immediately after the books arrived, the haunting began.

The case was actually investigated by a professional ghost-hunting team. One of the members of this team was Kayte Johnson, who said, "The trouble started when these books arrived. There were six books. They were all hard back and they arrived in a box, delivered by UPS. The guy walked it in, and he said, 'I'm glad I'm getting rid of this box.'

"And Gary said, 'Why is that?'

"The UPS man said, 'Because things have been happening on my truck ever since we put this box on my truck. There have been some really way-out far-out things.'

"Gary said, 'What kind of things?'

"He said, 'Things moving on their own. I'm having a hard time getting my truck to start…I can't explain it. I'm just glad that this box is not on my truck anymore.'

"And the guy left. The guy got on his truck...the truck started right up and the guy shot out."

Gary and Linda unpacked the box. They looked at each other before opening the box. Inside were these books for this woman. Said Kayte, "And they said, 'Oh, Lord... what have we done?'

"They called the woman and she said, 'Well, I'm going out of town. I won't be back for a couple of weeks, so if you could just hold on to them for me, I'll be there as soon as I can.'"

Gary and Linda agreed to hold the books until the lady returned, but, from the very beginning, unusual events began to occur. In fact, over the next two weeks, so many unusual events occurred that they actually considered burning the books.

One of the first events involved a strange cold spot in the back of the store. Initially both Linda and Gary didn't pay much attention to it and just assumed that there was a draft, but it was strange because they had never had any problems with the temperature before. Furthermore, the mysterious draft had no obvious cause, and seemed to be coming from nowhere.

Then came another event — a bizarre ghostly manifestation that is relatively rare, but still known among ghost researchers. This particular manifestation involves doors that suddenly — and for no known reason — cannot be opened.

Says Kayte, "They had a small little bathroom area, no shower or anything, just a commode and a sink, and a little bookcase that she had little decorative items in, and then a window that looked out into the alley area. And she had painted it a blue color, and put stars and clouds and everything. And this old door had this old metal doorknob on it."

They never had any problems with the door, but then one day, Linda went into the bathroom and she could not get out. No matter how many times she tried, the door would not open.

This particular door had wider gaps than most doors — so wide, in fact, that Linda could easily see where the doorknob latch was supposed to stick out and catch against the doorframe. However, there was nothing there. Says Linda, "I'm looking thinking maybe the doorknob broke."

This discovery, of course, only deepened the mystery. Something was holding the door closed and, if it wasn't the doorknob, then what was it? At one point, Linda pressed her ear against the door. She was shocked at what she heard.

"When I leaned up against the door, I could hear breathing," says Linda.

Needless to say, this frightened her. She called out to her husband, shouting, "I can't get out. You've got to come let me out."

Says Kayte, "She was stuck in the bathroom for two hours. He had to call a locksmith because he couldn't get her out, and when the locksmith arrived, he had knelt down, was getting ready to take a look at the doorknob, and there was a click. He didn't touch anything, hadn't touched anything yet. There was a click, and the door opened all by itself; she was sitting on the commode. In fact, he was in the way of the door opening, and he actually fell back because the door opened. He says, 'Lady, did you open the door?'

"'No, I didn't,' she said, adding, 'We have a ghost of some sort. I don't care what you think. There have been too many things going on.'"

It was shortly after this incident that yet another unexplained event occurred. Says Kayte, "She was in the store one day. Gary had a doctor's appointment, and she was in the shop by herself during the week when she said she felt somebody come and put their hand on her shoulders and put them around her neck. She said, 'They were squeezing, but I could still breathe.' And she said, 'I started praying. I got my gusto up and told it to release me or I was going to send it into the light.' She said she could feel it release, back on to her shoulders, and then it left."

After this incident, both Gary and Linda became convinced that a ghost was haunting their bookshop. The only explanation they could come up with was the presence of the books on black magic. It was at this point that they considered burning the books, but the events weren't over with yet. Around this time, they began to have problems with a large antique mirror that they had recently purchased and hung on the wall of their bookshop.

Says Kayte, "They had this mirror hanging on the wall in one of the book sections. And it was wooden, kind of a sun-rim around it, but it was just a round mirror. She said anytime she would walk by there, she felt as though that mirror was another portal. She never had a problem with the mirror. She thought it was really neat and would be great in the bookshop. They hung it up on the wall because that was the only place that was big enough to house it. She said after those books arrived, it was like this mirror turned into some sort of a portal. She said, 'I couldn't walk by it.' She said she felt like there was this invisible energy that would come out and try and grab her. She said, 'I know it sounds crazy, but I know it isn't crazy. Whatever came with those books — it's attached to those books — was in our shop.'"

Finally, the customer came in and picked up the books. Both Gary and Linda were hopeful that now that the books were gone, they would finally have some peace. And at first, things seemed to quiet down. They soon learned, however, that their adventure wasn't over yet.

Whatever had come with the books seemed to be gone, but the large round mirror continued to cause weird problems. Linda had trouble explaining it, but she felt as though some sort of portal in the mirror had been opened up. Every time she walked by the mirror, she would feel a strange presence. Then, on one occasion, the "presence" became undeniable.

Says Kayte, "She was eating her lunch at the counter, and she said a blast of force hit her so hard, it knocked her off the seat, knocked her off the stool. This was after the books were gone. And she said she hit the floor so hard, she said that the wind was knocked out of her. This force just came at her... it was like an invisible wall that just came at her so fast. She said, 'I went flying. My soda fell over. My sandwich went flying.'

"But the next day, she had bruises all over her shoulder where she had been hit. They looked like hands. It looked like fingers. She said, 'I wouldn't be in there by myself.'"

Linda was so upset by this new development that she and Gary decided to seek outside help. They located a group of ghost hunters, which ended up being Kayte Johnson and her team; they started their investigation by interviewing witnesses and visiting the location.

Another person they thought might be able to help was the woman who they believed may have been responsible for bringing the ghost to their bookshop in the first place: the customer who had ordered the books on black magic. The result was more dramatic than they had bargained for.

Says Kayte, "They actually had this woman come back and do whatever it was that she did...she cast a spell or she did something. When she got there — this woman had only been in the store twice; the first time to order the book, the second time to pick up her books. She wasn't a regular customer. And this woman came back, and she walked around the bookstore. The owner didn't say anything about the mirror, but she walked up to it and she started doing this language. It wasn't Latin, it was a language of some sort, and she was standing right in front of the mirror. For about fifteen minutes, she put her hands all around the mirror, and after she was done, started to walk away and the mirror shattered. The mirror shattered. They had to take it off.

"The woman just walked away. She didn't even stop. She just kept walking by them," says Kayte. "She said, 'Burn the frame, and everything will be fine.'"

Following the visit from the customer, events in the bookshop seemed to quiet down. They burned the mirror frame as the customer had advised. Finally, the ghost was gone for good.

Kayte Johnson was a part of the ghost-hunting team for two years and says the haunted bookshop was one of the more interesting and colorful cases, partly because Kayte was able to experience some of the activity herself during their investigation.

"I was only there twice. Cold in the back... the bathroom door we saw stuck, but nobody was in there. We couldn't get it open. We looked through the gap and there was nothing holding it. And the mirror...it really set my teeth on edge. It was beautiful. The frame was gorgeous, but I didn't want to get near the mirror. It was like this mirror was throwing this negative energy at you. It was like some sort of a portal, or a window, or a door, that when these books arrived, there was some sort of a connection to it, and it opened it up. It was really something. The mirror...you could feel it."

Thankfully, the haunting appears to be over. The bookshop has since closed down and the former owners have retired. However, in the same location there is now a tattoo parlor.

Chapter Thirteen

"Is That You, Gran?"

It was the early 1970s, and Eric Bleau was in third grade. He lived with his mother and grandmother in a three-bedroom home in the suburbs of Fountain Valley, located in Orange County, just south of Los Angeles.

Ever since he could remember, Eric's grandmother, Clara (pseudonym), suffered from ill health. She was diagnosed with emphysema and had lived with the condition for many years. Eric was very close to her and they would spend many hours together talking in her bedroom, which was adjacent to Eric's bedroom.

Eric's grandmother knew that her condition was deteriorating and she told Eric's mother, Joan (pseudonym), that her only request was that they not put her in a nursing home. Joan agreed, although this meant that practically all of her time and energy was spent taking care of her. They lived this way for many years, but by the time Eric reached the third grade, his grandmother's condition had worsened dramatically. She now began to suffer frequent bouts of dementia. She had weird emotional outbursts and often didn't recognize Eric or his mother. When she started having gastrointestinal bleeding and was experiencing hallucinations, Joan made one of the most difficult decisions of her life and put Clara in a rest home.

Clara was extremely upset and cursed up a storm as she was carted away to the rest home. Their extended family was furious and, with little knowledge of how difficult it was for Joan, condemned her decision. Needless to say, Eric's mother became consumed with guilt and began to second-guess her decision.

It was only a few days after Clara had been put in the rest home that Eric woke up one morning to an incredible sight: his grandmother was standing at the foot of his bed.

"She looked solid. There was a faint glow. I could make out her features better than I should have in that kind of lighting, but she did look absolutely solid… She looked like she was in better health."

"At first I thought, now that's just weird. She's not supposed to be here. She's in a nursing home. And when it finally clicked to me, she really isn't supposed to be here, all she did was smile at me. And then, the only way I can describe it, is almost like she became thousands of little particles and just kind of floated up to the ceiling and dispersed. And then I realized, 'Oh, my God. She's dead. She died.'"

Eric jumped out of bed and ran to tell his mother what happened. He went over to his mom's bedroom door and knocked on it, waking her up. She came to the door and opened it, wondering why her son had woken her up so early in the morning. Eric was about to say, "Mom, Gran's dead," when the phone rang.

Before he could say anything, Joan picked up the phone. It was the nursing home telling her that Granny had just passed away. She set down the phone and began crying. She turned to Eric and said, "Granny's just passed away."

Eric looked at her solemnly and said, "I know...she was just in my room."

His mother looked at him with a shocked expression, but Eric was insistent. He had seen his grandmother's ghost. "She looked solid," says Eric. "There was a faint glow. I could make out her features better than I should have in that kind of lighting, but she did look absolutely solid. She looked better than the last time I saw her alive, but she still looked around the same age. She looked like she was in better health."

Little did Eric know, but his experiences with his grandmother's spirit were only just beginning. Following her death, they cleared out her room and began to use it for storage.

Eric immediately discovered that he disliked being in his grandmother's former room. Before, when she was alive, he used to spend countless hours there, but now the room seemed creepy and spooky. He sometimes felt like he could still sense her presence there.

Then weird things began to happen. One early incident involved a box. Eric's mother confronted him one day and asked him why he was moving the boxes around in the storage room. Eric denied doing so, but his mother said that somebody had moved a box from the bed into the closet. Eric insisted it wasn't him.

This type of event happened several times. On each occasion, Eric's mom would accuse him of moving things around and tell him to stay out of the room, that he had no business in there. "I'm not," Eric would insist, denying the accusations.

After many such incidents, his mom became angry and decided to put a lock on the door. Despite this, objects continued to move in the room by themselves.

The events didn't stop there. Before she died, Eric's grandmother was deathly afraid of thunderstorms. Whenever there was thunder and lightning, she would stay up all night in her room with the lights on. After she died, whenever there was a thunderstorm, weird things would happen. Says Eric, "There would be many times — any time there was a thunder and lightning storm — that the door would be closed and locked in the middle of the night, and that light would come on by itself. Any kind of thunderstorm... and those lights would be on."

Eric had long ago decided that his grandma was still hanging around, but his mother remained skeptical. It was this particular ghostly manifestation that finally convinced Eric's mother that something strange was happening. The first few times she assumed that Eric had found a way to pick the locks, but when it kept happening even while Eric was sound asleep, she finally accepted that something was going on.

They talked about it. Eric was intrigued and his mother said she was fine with it...just as long as she never actually saw anything.

Things went on this way for a while, and Eric and his mother learned to live with the manifestations. Then eventually, the day came when they decided to move. Eric suddenly discovered that he was upset. He had grown used to having his grandmother's spirit in the house and realized that he was going to miss her. Although she had only manifested to him one time — on the morning she died — it still felt like she had often been there, quietly watching over them. He wondered: would his grandmother stay with the house or would she move with them?

It was shortly before they were due to move that Eric had a series of profound experiences with his grandmother's spirit. Says Eric, "I came home from school and I was usually at home by myself for an hour until my mom came home... I remember coming in, going to the bathroom, and doing my duty. And since my grandma had emphysema, she had a very, very distinct cough. I was sitting there, and I heard this cough. And automatically my ears perked up. I was like, whoa! It really freaked me out. Then I heard the cough walking down the hallway, and I heard it go into the bathroom behind me, and then it stopped. So I just sat there, and thought, 'Oh, my gosh!'"

Eric was so freaked out by the encounter, that he remained in the bathroom with the door closed until his mother came home. When he heard her finally arrive, he began screaming for her.

"Mom," he said, "I heard Gran! She coughed and walked down the hallway."

His mom looked thoughtful and said, "Well, if it was Gran, she did not mean to scare you. She wouldn't do that, you know that."

"I know," Eric said, nodding his head, "but I heard her."

Eric was both scared and fascinated. The next day at school, he told his best friend, Jake (pseudonym), about his encounter. Jake was skeptical and told Eric, "Whatever." When Eric insisted that it really happened, Jake's response was, "Shut up."

Eric was not to be put off. He said, "Okay, fine. Come over to my house after school and we'll play some video games. I've got some video games on my computer."

Jake agreed. After school they went to Eric's house and began playing video games in the living room. They quickly became distracted and had forgotten about their original reason for the visit...and then *it* happened.

"All of a sudden, I heard the cough," says Eric, "and I looked over at him and he was white already. He looked at me and said, 'Huh?'

"I said, 'Yeah, you heard it!'

"And he said, 'Uh-huh.' He just sat there. He didn't want to move. We heard the cough again — and he took off out of the house. He just went zoom, right out the front the door."

At this point, Eric's mother was just coming home. "What are you guys doing?" she asked.

"It's Gran again," Eric said. "She frightened me."

Joan was not sure what to think. Part of her wondered if her son was exaggerating. However, another part believed what he was saying. She reassured him again, telling Eric, "She's not meaning to scare you."

The next day, Eric returned to school and was discussing the incident with Jake when their other friend Andy (pseudonym) heard them talking. Andy was skeptical, but this time Jake assured him it was real. "Yeah, we heard it," Jake told him.

Andy laughed. "No, you didn't!"

Eric had already convinced Jake to come to his house after school, so he told Andy that he should join them and see for himself. "He agreed. So the three of us are now playing video games on the computer," says Eric, "and the same thing happens. All three of us bolt out of the house. Finally my mom comes home to the three of us sitting on the curb."

Eric's mother looked at him and said, "Okay, this is enough. You are going to go tell Gran right now that she is scaring you." She grabbed him by the arm and led him into the house down into the hallway where the coughing noises had originated.

Eric felt a little strange, but, talking out loud, he said, "Gran, you're scaring me. You're scaring me a lot. Can you please stop?"

Eric didn't really expect a response, so he was shocked at what followed. "The next thing that happened — the best way I can describe it — is if somebody took all their thoughts, emotions, and feelings, packed it into a softball, and tossed it at me. It was like all of a sudden this surge of emotion and understanding and feelings just hit me. I broke down crying."

After he recovered, Eric explained to his mom what happened. He told her that Clara didn't understand why they were leaving and she didn't know if she would be able to follow them. Both Eric and his mother were shocked, but the confrontation seemed to work. The coughing noises stopped. Eric and his mother moved out of the house and into an apartment a short distance away.

The Dream....

Meanwhile, unknown to Eric, his mother was still consumed with guilt about her decision to place Clara in a nursing home. It wasn't long after they moved that she began having dreams about Clara. The dreams were always the same. Suddenly she would see Clara and the dream would become extraordinarily vivid, almost life-like. Clara would turn to her and say, "Joan, I need to talk to you." At this point, Joan usually woke up screaming. She was afraid that grandma was still angry with her, and the last thing she wanted to do was argue with her ghost.

Meanwhile, Eric also began to have dreams about Clara. In the dream, he suddenly saw his grandmother sitting across the table from him. "And then at some point in the dream, she reached across the table and touched my hand and said, 'Eric, I must talk to you,'" says Eric.

"At that point, the dream changed. It was like no longer a dream. It was like a vivid reality. It was no longer hazy. I thought, 'Am I still dreaming?' She touched me and said, 'I must talk to you.' The dream changed, but the room changed too. It was like we weren't anywhere...it was all dark except for this light above the table. She asked me how I was doing at school, asked me about how everything was going, what I was doing, how did I break my arm. And she said, 'Well, I've got to go, but I want you to tell your mom something. It is very important. Just tell her I need to talk to her. Please I need to speak with her.'"

At this point, Eric woke up. The next morning, he went up to his mother and said, "Mom, I had a dream last night I want to tell you about."

"What?" she asked.

"Well, it involved Gran."

Joan was shocked and nearly lost her balance. "What happened?" she asked.

Eric explained the dream and told her, "She said she really needed to talk to you."

Joan was amazed, but kept her feelings hidden from her son. She hadn't yet told him about her own dreams. Meanwhile, her dreams returned with a vengeance. Her mother was coming to her in her dreams practically every night. On each occasion, Joan would wake up terrified.

Then, finally, Joan overcame her fear and confronted her mother in the dream state. Joan found herself in a dream again hearing Clara's voice calling for her. "Joan, please stop," she said. "Just talk to me."

"Okay, what?" Joan said.

Joan was amazed at what happened next. Her mother approached her and explained that she was not mad at her, and that she understood why she had to place her in a nursing home. She wasn't angry, and she was now feeling fine. She then told her daughter that an envelope had come in the mail and that Joan had to open it. "It's very important," she explained. "You cannot put it off."

Joan woke up. Like the other dreams, this one was extremely vivid and realistic, and it felt like she had truly been in Clara's presence. Recalling Clara's insistent instructions in the dream, Joan went hunting for the unopened letter.

After a short search, she found the letter, which had somehow been ignored and pushed aside due to Joan's busy schedule. The letter was from an organization that was providing them with funds for having taken on the duties of caring for the ailing Clara at her home instead of putting her in a hospital. The letter explained that there had been a class-action lawsuit against this organization, which had allegedly been miscalculating the appropriation of funds to the various deserving families, including theirs. According to the letter, there were only a few days left to respond. Joan quickly responded. The end result was that they were owed a large amount of money, which came at a time when it was badly needed.

Time went on. Clara's spirit finally seemed to be at peace, and for many years there were no further incidents.

Still a Haunting Presence....

One day when he was in Junior High, Eric was riding his bicycle past his old house when he saw one of the girls who lived there playing in the front yard. He stopped his bike and told the girl, "You know, I used to live here."

The girl looked at him and said, "So, you know about the old lady."

"What old lady?" Eric asked.

"The old lady who sits in the rocking chair."

Eric was shocked. His grandmother used to sit for hours in her rocking chair, rocking back and forth, by the entryway of her room. "What room do you have?" he asked.

The girl explained the location of her room, which was the same as Clara's. Eric wasn't surprised at this revelation. "Well, where is the rocking chair?" he asked.

"Right at the door," the girl said.

"Does it frighten you?" he asked her.

"No," she replied. "She's just sometimes there at night."

Eric decided it was time to reveal the truth. He told the girl, "You don't need to be afraid of her. That's my great-grandmother. She'll never hurt you."

A Guardian Angel....

Eric grew up and, at age twenty, got married. Shortly later, his wife became pregnant. During this time, Eric told his wife about his encounters with his grandmother's spirit. To his dismay, his wife did not want to hear about them. In fact, she became so upset and frightened that she insisted on sleeping with the lights on for the next two weeks. Eric learned to keep silent.

His grandmother, however, had a different plan. Eric suddenly and occasionally began to sense her presence in their new apartment in Yorba Linda. On a few occasions, he woke up and saw shadows moving around in the hallway. Strangely, he didn't feel frightened, but was instead comforted by the presence. He felt certain that it was his grandmother, probably checking up on their upcoming baby.

At this point, neither he nor his wife knew if they were going to have a boy or a girl. They planned to wait for the birth and make it a surprise. Then Eric had another dream about his grandmother. She approached him and said, "Don't be afraid, it's just me. I know you saw me. Don't be afraid. I'm not meaning to scare you. I'm hoping I'm not."

In the dream, Eric replied, "I had a feeling it might be you."

"I'm here to watch over your daughter for you."

Eric didn't tell his wife about the dream. "She would have laid eggs!" Eric explained. Instead, he just hung a small-framed photograph of Clara in the nursery. A few months later, his wife gave birth to a healthy baby girl.

That was the last time Eric was visited by his grandmother. Eric's case is a good example of a spirit that manifested for a purpose — to complete unfinished business. However, it turned out not to be Eric's last experience with ghosts. His next experience would involve a haunting of a very different kind.

Chapter Fourteen

"My House is Haunted!"

"The house we live in now definitely has a presence," Eric Bleu said about his home located in Yorba Linda, in Orange County, just south of Los Angeles. Eric was no stranger to ghosts. Because of his experiences with his grandmother's spirit, he was already convinced that ghosts were real.

Still, he was surprised when he discovered that the house he had had decided to move into also turned out to be haunted. He had divorced his wife and was now seeing and falling in love with another woman, Patricia, whom he would soon marry. It was her home, and Eric moved in not long after they met.

It was shortly after they met that Eric had his first experience in their home. Patricia was with him as they both sat on the couch in the living room, watching television. Patricia's pet cat, Peaches, was also in the living room with them.

As they watched their program, they suddenly became distracted by Peaches, who began growling behind the couch. They stood up and looked at the cat. Its hackles were raised along its back, and it stared at a certain spot behind the couch, adjacent to the archway to the dining room, paralyzed with fear.

"Peaches, what's the matter with you?" Patricia asked and reached out to sooth her pet. The cat growled loudly the moment she reached out.

Eric and Patricia looked at the spot where the cat was staring. They turned back to the cat. "There's nothing there," Eric said.

He became curious and decided to examine the spot more closely. That's when he got a real shock. Says Eric, "I walked over there, trying to line up where he was staring. I walked over there...

and there was a huge cold spot right there. It was ice-cold. I looked at my wife and said, 'There's a very cold spot right here.' And about the time I said that, the cold spot started moving. It jumped off my body going towards the back door and the other side of the archway. I could feel this column of cold go right through the room. And I looked at the cat, and the cat was tracking it. He saw it and he was watching it."

Patricia corroborates Eric's testimony. As she says, "The cat saw something. His hair and tail raised and he was really rigid. We knew something was up because he was so freaked out."

After a few moments, the cold spot was gone, and the cat stopped growling. The incident, however, impressed both Eric and Patricia. Whatever it was, it didn't seem hostile or evil. Instead, it had a benevolent feel about it. It seemed pretty clear to them that some type of ghost was responsible, and both Eric and Patricia had a pretty good idea who it might be.

As it turned out Patricia did know a little bit about the home's history. It was built in the 1950s. By coincidence, as a little girl, Patricia's mom was best friends with a girl whose parents owned the house. Patricia's uncle (her mom's brother) was also a friend of the family that originally owned the home. According to Patricia's uncle, sometime in the earlier history of the house, somebody had sat on the couch in the living room, put a shotgun to his head, and killed himself. Whenever her uncle came over, he would mention the incident, and point to the section of the wall where the bullet went, right by the archway to the dining room — exactly where the cat had been staring. So after the incident with Peaches, Eric and Patricia wondered if they were dealing with the ghost of the man who committed suicide.

At first it appeared to be an isolated incident. However, it wasn't long before both Patricia and Eric were experiencing other strange events.

Shortly after the original owners purchased the house, they built a laundry room behind the garage and converted the garage into another bedroom. So now when Eric had to do his laundry, he had to walk through this bedroom to get to the laundry room. Each time he walked through the room, he had the strangest feeling that he was intruding on somebody, like he was being watched, or like he didn't belong there.

"If I have to go into the laundry room at night, I try to make it as fast as possible," says Eric, adding, "Not that I'm scared."

Patricia also reported similar feelings. Both of them wondered if their ghost was "living" in the converted bedroom.

As time went on, the haunting slowly escalated. The ghost became braver and more active, manifesting in a variety of ways.

One very common experience for both Eric and Patricia was seeing a shadowy apparition flit by in their peripheral vision. It happened so many times that there was no question that something unusual was going on. Says Eric, "I'd be laying on the couch watching TV, and out of the corner of my eye I'd see someone walk out of the hallway and into the kitchen, kind of a shadow. I'd turn my head and there'd be nobody there. My wife sits in the reclining chair kind of in front of the couch a little bit, facing towards the TV. She said she'd see things moving out of the corner of her eye in the living room. A lot of it is focused in the front living room."

Adds Patricia, "My recliner sits facing the television in the living room. It makes me laugh because every time I see it, I automatically look to see who's in the living room. And I think, 'Why do I do that? I know what's going on!'"

Another type of manifestation that occurred on numerous occasions involved objects that would be moved from their original location or would disappear altogether. As Eric says, "We have things that disappear and reappear."

A typical incident involved one of Patricia's belongings. One day Patricia turned to Eric and asked him, "Did you move my box?" She had recently purchased a small box to hold her sewing equipment. She always kept the box on the sewing table behind the couch, near the archway.

Eric looked over at the sewing table. The sewing box was gone. "No," he replied. "Why would I move your box?"

They searched everywhere, but the sewing box was nowhere to be found. A few days later, Patricia was walking through the living room when she looked down — and there was the box, sitting on the bench next to the sewing table. She looked down at the box and then at Eric. "Did you put this here? Did you find it?"

"I walked over there, and there was a huge cold spot right there. It was ice-cold. I looked at my wife and I said, 'There's a very cold spot right here.' And about the time I said that, the cold spot started moving."

"No," Eric replied, and raised his eyebrows at Patricia with a knowing glance. They both knew what had happened. The ghost had done it.

"I think our friend is playing with us," says Eric, adding that many similar incidents have happened. "I had a pair of flip-flops and I couldn't find one of them. We tore the house apart looking for it. We could not find it. It was nowhere to be found. Then about a week or two later, it reappeared in the middle of the room, sitting there. It was kind of like, 'Hey, were you looking for this?'"

They normally take off their shoes upon entering the house and keep them by the door, so the disappearance of the shoe was particularly baffling.

Patricia confirms the incident. "We looked under the couches, under the furniture, trying to find this other shoe. We tore everything apart; in the closets, in the bedrooms...everywhere we had gone to where we might have misplaced it. We tore the house apart. And about two weeks later, it was laying right out in the middle of the living room floor. It was like, 'Where did that come from?' He does silly things like that, so he's got a sense of humor."

Another manifestation is the powerful feeling of a presence. Both Eric and Patricia have felt this feeling very strongly on many occasions. Patricia says that she often senses his presence when she is changing her clothes. As she says, "There have been numerous times that I've had a feeling of being watched, and I've caught things out of the corner of my eye. It's one of those things where you never see it, but you always see it out of your peripheral vision. You always see something in passing."

While she still feels the ghost is benevolent, she admits that she thinks he also has a voyeuristic side. But, says Patricia jokingly, "I don't care. Let him get his jollies."

One common activity performed by ghosts is the switching on and off of light switches. Eric and Patricia's ghost also performed this activity constantly, but only with one particular light — a halogen lamp on a long pole that they had placed in the living room near the archway. Although they turned off all the lights in the house each evening before bed, when they woke up in the morning, this particular lamp would often be turned back on.

"I'd ask Eric, 'Did you turn this light on?'" says Patricia. "This was before we realized that he — *our friend* — was doing it. And Eric would say, 'No.' That light was always on. Every morning I'd walk into the room and that light would be on in there."

On a few occasions, they have had guests over who also experienced an encounter with their active, friendly ghost. On one such occasion, they had two friends over, a couple, who were somehow both skeptical and afraid. After Eric and Patricia revealed that they had a ghost, the woman became frightened and said, "I don't want to see it."

The man, however, was not afraid, or at least, behaved in a way that attempted to put on the appearance of confidence. He laughed and began to speak out loud to the ghost, taunting it by saying, "Oh, you stay in that room. We don't want to see you, you just stay in there." He repeated it several times until his girlfriend finally told him to stop. "Don't taunt him," she complained. "I don't want it to appear. I don't want to see it."

Apparently, this attention was enough — Patricia speculates — to irritate and evoke the ghost into a response. Shortly after the conversation, the toilet in the back of the house flushed by itself.

All four witnesses looked at each other — Patricia and Eric with knowing expressions; their friends with expressions of surprise and fear. The woman turned slightly pale. Throughout the evening, the toilet flushed several times, something it does not normally do.

By the end of the evening, both their friends were convinced that the house was, in fact, haunted — a conclusion Patricia and Eric had long ago reached.

Again, Eric and Patricia were pretty sure that they knew the identity of the ghost, but it wasn't until Eric's close childhood friend came over that they received independent confirmation. Eric's friend John (pseudonym) was in the army and was not often available for visits, so when he called and told Eric that he was going to be in the Los Angeles area, Eric insisted that he come to visit their home and meet his wife, whom he had never met.

John agreed, and arrived the next night. Patricia was out of the house at school, so Eric and John had plenty of time to catch up. Soon the conversation turned to Eric and Patricia's house. Eric said, "You know, we've got a ghost."

"Really?" said John. "You know I'm sensitive to these things."

"Really?" said Eric, and remembered that, when they were kids, John had often mentioned that he saw strange things. Eric then asked John if he might be able to sense anything about their ghost.

John agreed to try, and explained to Eric what he was going to do. "Get me a pad of paper and a pencil, and just let me walk through the house and I'll write down stuff. And I'll come back and I'll tell you what I think."

"Okay, fair enough," Eric agreed. He found a pad of paper and a pencil and gave them to John. As John began his walk-through of the house, Eric quietly followed behind. Says Eric, "I trailed him because I wanted to see where he went."

The first place John went to was the bedroom that had been converted from the garage. "This is his room," John said. "He likes this room."

It was the same room that both Eric and Patricia had often felt the ghost's presence. Eric kept his surprise a secret as John continued the walk-through. They next went into the kitchen.

"This kitchen used to be smaller," John said. "Did you know that? This kitchen used to be smaller."

"I don't know," Eric shook his head. He didn't know, but he later asked Patricia and she told him that, yes, there used to be an island in the center of the kitchen, but they removed it because it had made the kitchen too small.

John walked into the living room and paused in the area of the couch. He looked around and said, "This is definitely an add-on. It was not originally here."

Again, John was right. They next walked into the backyard, where John began to sense more events that turned out to be true. "I sense kids," he said. "I sense that the back fence used to be shorter and it was a chain-link. And I sense that there was somebody telling the kids not to climb over the fence. I sense plates in the dirt. There were plates in the dirt, somehow."

Eric was definitely impressed. Again John was correct. A woman who formerly lived in the home had used the backyard as a daycare center. She also had what Patricia called "an unusual sense of decoration" and would use plates as planters for the flowers she grew in the backyard.

They walked back into the house. Eric couldn't wait to hear what his friend would say next.

"Your ghost is a him," John said. "It's definitely a him and he died in this house."

Another direct hit, thought Eric.

John walked back into the converted bedroom, stood there for a few moments with a puzzled expression, and then walked back into the living room. He walked right up to the wall where there was a small piece of plaster removed. He felt the wall and looked at Eric with a strange expression.

That particular wall was shared with the master bedroom, which was on the other side. John quickly walked into the master bedroom and began feeling the other side of the same wall.

"This is weird," he said. "I feel something very strong here. But it's not at this side of the wall, and it's not coming from the other side of the wall. It's inside the wall."

"What?" Eric asked.

"It's something small," John said, still feeling the wall. "It's a teeny, little, small thing."

John stopped feeling the wall and looked at Eric. "Did someone shoot a shotgun here?"

"Are you kidding me?" Eric asked.

John shook his head. "No, I think there might be buckshot in the wall."

Eric nodded and explained the story. "Tricia's uncle used to tell us that a guy committed suicide by setting off a shotgun into the wall."

John nodded. "Yep, that's what it is."

John continued to walk through the house, amazing Eric with his accuracy of past events. He pointed to a spot and said that a piano used to sit there. He looked outside the window, pointed to a particular spot, and said that there used to be a big tree there with Christmas lights on it.

Eric told John that he was right on both accounts, and asked John if he knew anything more about the ghost and why he had killed himself.

John said that he wasn't sure of the exact reason, but he got the impression that the man had gotten into an argument with his wife about children and as a result had become so emotionally upset that he sat down on the couch in the living room, took a shotgun, and blew his head off.

John wasn't able to sense any other information, but what he had sensed was enough confirmation for both Eric and Patricia. Everything John had said was correct. Although they still didn't know the exact identity of the ghost, it was clear to both of them that the story their uncle used to joke about was, in fact, no joke. It really happened. And they had to live with the consequences. Their house was haunted.

Activity continues to happen in their home on a fairly regular basis. They both believe that their new two-year-old baby is also seeing the ghost. Says Patricia, "Eric and I talked about it and we think the baby sees him because the baby will look over our shoulders or towards the kitchen area, or the back of the couch and start grinning and smiling. She'll start laughing at something, and there's nothing there."

All the ghostly activity doesn't scare them in the slightest. Says Patricia, "It doesn't bother me in the least that this is happening. It's never been a threat. As long as he's not going to harm us in any way, it's fine. I don't mind having him around. I think it's interesting, the different things. It makes me laugh because you never know what to expect."

Eric is also fine with living in a haunted house. Neither of them is interested in having paranormal groups come in to "cleanse" their home of spirits. Instead, they have learned to live with the ghost and its little pranks. Strange events continue to occur, but when they do, it's nothing more than a little reminder that like many people across the world, they are living in a haunted house.

"You kind of just don't want to believe what you think is going on. You look for some real logical explanation, like we have toxic air, so it was interesting living there... Of course, these are the things they don't tell you when you rent a place."

Chapter Fifteen

The Buena Park Ghost

It had been a long day. It was July 1974, and Carol and Jim Ross had just moved into their new rental home in Buena Park. The home was previously occupied by personnel from a nearby military base, but they had all moved out suddenly, leaving the house available to rent for Carol and Jim and their three kids; Jonny (age ten), Donna (age seven), and Sam (age four). *[Note: the children's names are pseudonyms.]* Although it wasn't a large home — about 1,300 square feet — it had four bedrooms, which meant that each child could have their own bedroom. It also had one of the biggest yards in the neighborhood, which was great for the kids. It was close to Jim's job; he worked the nightshift at Southern California Edison. It seemed to be the perfect find.

There were a few strange things about the house that, at the time, didn't seem significant, but would later come to haunt them. Whoever had lived there before had moved out quickly, and still left odds and ends in the house. One of them was an old Ouija board that was hanging on a wall in the entryway. Another strange thing was one of the bedrooms, which was painted a depressing and odd-colored battleship gray-green, had a pentagram drawn on the floor.

A final odd thing was that the owners had left their dog, an Irish Setter, complete with authentic papers. However, Carol understood that they were in the Navy and unable to care for the dog, and since the kids seemed to like him, they decided to keep him.

A crowd of their friends showed up and helped them move in. By the end of the day, they had all the furniture and boxes in the house. Their friends went home, and Jim went to take a nap to catch some sleeping time before midnight, when he had to wake up and go to work.

Donna and Sam decided that they didn't want their own room, but would rather share. They picked a room and set up the bunk beds. Donna was older and slept on the top bunk while Sam took the bottom.

It was bedtime for Donna and Sam so Carol tucked them into their beds, kissed them each goodnight, and then walked across the hallway to her oldest son's room to check on him. Suddenly, four-year-old Sam started screaming.

"My oldest son and I ran in there, and Sam was on the bed, and he was screaming, 'It's got me! It's got me! Help me! I can't get up!'" says Carol.

As a mother, Carol could see that her son was obviously terrified of something. Visibly, however, nothing seemed wrong. Then she reached down to pick Sam up. "He's this little, tiny, parakeet-type child, small and all of about forty-five pounds — and I could not lift him off the bed," says Carol.

Meanwhile, Carol's husband woke up and came rushing into the room. "What's wrong?!" he asked.

Carol looked at him with frustration. "I can't get Sam off the bed!"

"It's got me! It's got me!" Sam continued to scream at the top of his lungs, crying.

Carol stepped back to let her husband pick up Sam. "Jim, who is six foot four and 240 pounds, he went over and he couldn't get him off the bed," says Carol.

Then, only a few seconds later, it was over. Whatever was keeping Sam glued to the bed suddenly released him. Sam stopped crying. In fact, it suddenly became apparent to both Jim and Carol that he didn't seem to remember any of it. He began behaving as if nothing unusual had happened.

Jim and Carol, however, were mystified. After talking about it, they decided that Sam must be having nightmares, or "night-terrors," which wouldn't be unusual for a growing and hyperactive four-year-old boy. Never mind that there was no explanation for them being unable to unglue Sam from his bed.

Later that night, Jim went to work while Carol continued to unpack. Steve (pseudonym), a friend of Jim's, arrived to help Carol work through the night to move in. While they unpacked,

Carol explained to Steve what had happened with Sam earlier that evening.

"We were sitting on the floor in the living room and all of a sudden the radio turns on, and we haven't even gotten any radios unpacked, let alone plugged in," says Carol.

Both of them looked at each other in shock. That was enough for Carol. She was convinced that they were dealing with an actual ghost. She quickly called her husband at work. She spilled out the story and said, "I want to move out! Now! We're still packed. This will be no problem."

Jim, of course, was shocked, and tried to convince her that there was no ghost. He also pointed out that they obviously couldn't afford to move out.

"I don't care if we don't have the money! I want to move out."

"We're not moving out," Jim repeated. He told her to wait, that he would be home soon, and they would figure things out.

Carol hung up the phone. She and Steve looked up at the Ouija board. Obviously, it would have to go. Carol looked over at Steve.

"I'll get rid of it," he said. The board, which was made of wood, had somehow turned an unpleasant shade of green. Steve stepped forward and removed it from the wall. He then took it outside and threw it away into the flood channel across the street...far from Carol and Jim's home.

The incident had left Carol unnerved and she was eager for her husband to get back home. Little did she know that the haunting had only just begun.

The next incident occurred a few days later. They had a standing fan that they had owned for at least a couple years. Suddenly, and for no reason, Sam walked forward as if in a trance and stuck his fingers into the fan. His loud screams alerted everyone.

Thankfully, he wasn't badly hurt, only scared. "Why did you do that?" Carol asked.

"I don't know," Sam replied meekly. "I just did."

A few days later, another strange event occurred, also involving Sam. Says Carol, "We had a wading pool out in the front yard, and he fell into it face first and couldn't get out. I mean this water didn't even go up to his ankles." Carol had to rush forward and physically lift him out of the pool. Thankfully, she was able to do so.

By this point, however, it was obvious to her that whatever ghost was haunting her house, it seemed to be picking mostly on Sam.

Then there was the dog. From the very first day, the dog was, as Carol says, "weird." The only real problem was the barking. The dog barked incessantly, but the strange thing was that the dog would only bark at one particular corner in the living room, as if there was something there that nobody else could see.

It was no better if they put the dog outside. The minute they put him outside, the dog ran over to one particular section of fence on the edge of the backyard and continued to bark. Every time it was the same thing. Not surprisingly, complaints from the neighbors came in and they had to keep the dog inside.

Another event that occurred not long after they moved in involved strange sounds coming from the roof. The first time it occurred Carol was feeding the kids in the dining room. Suddenly, the sound of heavy footsteps stomping on the roof came from above.

"What is that?" Jonny asked.

Sam and Donna also looked to their mother for an answer.

"Well, it's just the trees on the house," she said. "Don't worry about it."

Carol, of course, knew that there were no trees. It was the ghost. However, she wasn't sure how the kids felt about it, and she didn't want to scare them.

A week or so later, Jim was in the house when he heard somebody walking up the stairs and also what sounded like somebody handling metal chains. The only problem, he was alone in the house — and there were no chains on the premises.

The incidents continued. After they were finally moved in, the children wanted to take advantage of their big front yard and go outside to play. Because it was summer, they left the front door open, leaving only the unlocked screen door. However, when the kids came back in from playing, they couldn't get in. The screen door was locked. They knocked, rang the doorbell, and screamed for their mom to let them in.

She saw the kids clustered by the front door, "Why aren't you coming in?"

"The screen door's locked."

"Well, don't lock it when you go out."

"We didn't," the kids protested.

Carol, disbelieving, told them, "Just try to pay attention to what you're doing."

The next time the kids went out to play, the same thing happened. The front door was locked, and the kids couldn't get in. Again, Carol blamed the kids for locking themselves out. Again, her children protested, saying they left the door unlocked.

After it happened a third, fourth, and fifth time, Carol finally realized what was happening. Throughout the year, the kids would be locked out of the house dozens of times.

Sam, in particular, seemed to be singled out the most for this activity. By now Carol had decided that their ghost was a poltergeist and that it was picking on Sam because he was the youngest and most vulnerable and couldn't defend himself. It was no surprise to her that Sam would be locked out of the house almost every time he ventured outside.

The strange occurrences continued. The next really big unexplained event occurred on Thanksgiving evening. Sam had a major temper-tantrum and ran into his room and slammed the door.

This had happened before, but this time, something very bizarre happened. Sam became locked in his room, unable to open the door. The door had no lock. In fact, it didn't even have a latch of any kind. The doorknob was fixed and the door opened and closed by applying light pressure.

Sam called out that he was stuck in his room. Carol and Jim didn't believe him until they tried to open the door themselves. To their shock, they were unable to open the door. No matter how hard they tried, the door would not open. The only solution they could think of was to take the door off the hinges. The room had a window, but it wasn't the kind that opened.

They didn't have any tools, so they went next door and asked their neighbor if he had any tools to take a door off the hinges. He did and graciously agreed to help. He came over and surveyed the situation. He was unable to open the door and noted that the hinges could only be removed from inside the bedroom.

The neighbor went outside, broke the bedroom window, climbed in, and removed the door. Sam was finally able to exit his room.

A few days later, they put the door back on, and at first, everything was fine. Then one day, Sam began screaming that he was locked in his room again. This time, they were able to climb in through the newly replaced window that now opened and closed, and again removed the door.

A few days later, they put the door back on one more time. However, it wasn't long before the same thing happened. Although there was no apparent reason for it, Sam's bedroom door would not open. On this occasion, however, whatever was holding the door closed suddenly released. From that point on, Sam usually kept his door open. Whenever he closed it — more often than not — it would suddenly and mysteriously become stuck.

The Rosses slowly learned to live with their ghost. The first year was the most active. However, the next few years brought more activity and new paranormal manifestations.

Because of Jim's work schedule, both he and Carol were often awake deep into the night and early morning hours. They relished the time together, free from the constant interruptions and needs of their children. Unfortunately, their ghost had another thing in mind.

One evening, as they sat in the bedroom talking, the toilet in the master bathroom suddenly flushed by itself. Carol and Jim looked at each other in surprise and rushed into the bathroom. The toilet had definitely flushed — they could *see* the water swirling — but there was nobody there. An examination of the toilet revealed no abnormalities.

Just as they were trying to figure out the mystery, they heard the sound of the other toilet in the front bathroom flushing. They rushed over there in time to watch the water going down the drain. Again, nobody was there.

While they were in the front bathroom, they heard the sound of the master bathroom toilet flushing again. They ran over to it, and seconds later, the other toilet flushed again.

"It's the ghost," Carol said.

Jim nodded. What other explanation could there be? They sat down on the bed. The toilets continued to flush — first one and then the other — for the next five minutes. Finally it stopped.

At first they thought the toilet-flushing incident was a unique event. However, as the years passed, it would happen again and again. Each time it was the same. First one toilet would flush and then the other, says Carol, "over and over and over."

It wasn't long after the first toilet-flushing incident that Sam started having more problems with the poltergeist. One evening, he woke everyone in the house with his screaming. Carol rushed in to his bedroom. "What's the matter?" she asked.

"It's coming for me, mom! It's coming for me!"

"Well, what is coming for you, honey?" she asked, trying to sooth him.

"I don't know!" he cried. "I can't tell, but it's going to get me!"

Carol comforted Sam to the best of her ability. She told him that it was probably just a nightmare, and that nothing was going to get him. However, she wasn't convinced herself.

A few nights later, Sam woke up again, screaming for his life. Again, Carol tried to comfort him, but she felt powerless to do anything.

For the next six months, Sam woke up nearly every night with the "night terrors." Each time, he said that something was trying to get him. Each time, Carol told him it was just a nightmare, but with each incident, she became more and more convinced that the ghost was responsible.

Carol took Sam to a child psychologist, though even this didn't seem to help. On a few occasions, Sam would be so upset and afraid that Carol would let him sleep in her bed with Jim and her. She told this to the psychologist and he said that she should never do this, that it "would do Sam damage." Carol did her best to follow the advice, but she wasn't sure it was the best thing to do, considering the situation.

One particular "night terror" incident was especially bizarre. It was the middle of the night and Carol woke up to the familiar sound of Sam screaming in his bed. "Mom! Help! It's coming!"

She ran to his room and cradled him in her arms. "What's wrong?" she asked.

"It's going to come and get me!" Sam screamed, crying.

"What? What is?"

"Look, mom! It's right there!" Sam pointed next to the doorway, near the light-switch. "Look at it! It's going to come and get me!"

Carol looked to where Sam was pointing. Nothing was there.

She shook her son and looked into his eyes to make sure he was, in fact, awake and not sleepwalking. He appeared to be perfectly normal, except for the fact that he was terrified of something standing by the door. He refused to get out of bed and kept pointing and screaming, "Look, mom! It's going to come and get me!"

Carol went over and turned the light switch on and off. Everything appeared to be normal, at least to her. Sam, however, insisted that something was there. She had no doubt that her son was sincere.

"You could tell from his look that he saw something," says Carol. "He knew something was there."

As usual, Sam begged and pleaded to go and sleep with her in their bed. On this occasion, Carol relented and allowed him to sleep with them. Despite what the psychologist said, she was afraid that the ghost would do more damage to her son than she would.

Finally, one day the nightmares just stopped. Meanwhile, the ghost had found a new way to make its presence known. The latest activity involved just one type of paranormal manifestation: missing objects.

They weren't sure when it first started, perhaps shortly after they moved in, but it wasn't until later that it became a problem. Most often, it was the car keys. The first few times, Carol just brushed off the missing keys to forgetfulness. However, after it kept happening, she knew something was wrong. "I have one place I keep my car keys, but they would never be there. They'd be in the living room, they be in the bathroom — no place related," she said.

And of course, it wasn't just the car keys. Clothes, toys, shoes, dishes — "little things like that," says Carol. A few times, the missing items were extremely valuable. There was a small table in the kitchen that Carol used for her bills and paperwork. Whenever Jim received his paycheck, he would dutifully place it on the kitchen table so Carol could take care of it.

Typically the table was stacked with mounds of various papers and files. One morning, Jim came home and, as usual, placed his check on the kitchen table. Later, when Carol got ready to go to the bank, she looked for the check. It wasn't there. She searched the table several times, finally looking at each item separately, but the check was gone.

She told her husband who insisted that he had put the check there. For the next few hours, they tore the house apart. "We absolutely could not find it," says Carol.

Suddenly Sam said, "Look in the trash can, mom."

"It's already been emptied," she replied.

Carol looked at Jim with an expression of dread. They both simultaneously ran outside to the large trash bin. By coincidence, it was "garbage day" and the garbage truck was already visible a few blocks down the street, heading their way. Carol and Jim furiously began sifting through the garbage. Within a few minutes, they found the check. They looked at each other with pride: the ghost had tried to take their check, but they found it. This ghost was not going to beat them.

For Carol, it was a turning point. No longer would she let the ghost interfere with their lives. She went to the bank and deposited the check. That was the only time the ghost had ever taken their paycheck. Mostly, however, it was the keys.

By this time, the kids were well aware of the ghost. They called him George. Carol and Jim discussed the ghost with them and the children seemed fine with it. However, Carol warned them not to tell their teachers, and to be careful whom they told, as some people wouldn't understand. The kids understood. They told some of their friends, some of whom refused to come over. Together the kids decided that George lived in the closet in the green room with the pentagram.

The green room was also the focus of some unusual paranormal events. One day Carol walked into the room and was shocked at how cold it was. The vents must be clogged, she told herself. However, it happened many times, and each time, the temperature was dramatic enough that anybody who walked into the room noticed it. At first she didn't think much of it.

Then one day, a young lady came to visit. She explained th
she used to live in the house and that she had come back to r
the dog was still there. To her delight, he was. Carol allowd
to visit with the dog, and during that time, asked her iere.
ever experienced anything strange in the house while lior a
The lady nodded. She explained that she had livevents
while with her young daughter, but so many unex

had occurred that it forced them out of the house. She said that her room was the green room and that it was always ten degrees colder than the rest of the house. She declined to elaborate about any other strange events and quickly left.

As the years passed, the paranormal incidents happened with regular frequency, usually once or twice a month, with occasional slow-downs or flare-ups. Before they knew it, six years had passed and their oldest son Jonny was driving.

That was when the flare-up started. As a new driver, Jonny was eager to take every opportunity he could to get behind the wheel and be on the road. However, more often than not, when Jonny went to look for his keys, they would be missing.

Like his mom, Jonny tried to solve the problem by putting his keys in one particular location. Even that didn't work; the keys went missing so often that the situation quickly became intolerable. Carol finally came up with a plan. There was a closet in the hallway that had a padlock on it. Carol purchased a metal lockbox and placed it on a shelf. Each time Jonny came home, he placed his keys in the lockbox, locked the box, and then closed the hallway and locked it. That was the only way they were able to keep Jonny's car keys from disappearing. Strangely, the keys to the closet and the lockbox never disappeared.

Again, they felt proud; they had beaten the ghost at his own game. Throughout the years, the children occasionally changed rooms. For much of her time in the house, Donna's room was the green room. Ironically, she never had any real problems with the ghost, definitely not to the extent that her brothers did.

Eventually the kids grew up and moved out. The ghost, however, stayed. At the time, Carol was a social worker. One day she was working the crisis line when she befriended Greg (pseudonym), a gentleman who was down on his luck and needed a place to stay. With so nany empty rooms in her own home, Carol decided she would let e man stay until he was able to get back on his feet again.

At first, things were going well. Then one day, Greg suddenly ted out that he was locked in his room. As before, there was ical reason, and the door remained mysteriously glued shut. hey had to take it off the hinges.

It was then that Carol learned that Greg was taking drugs. She told him that he wasn't allowed to take drugs while in her home, and then told him about the ghost, and that it was the one who locked him in his room — that the ghost was angry at him for smoking weed.

That seemed to do the trick; Greg stopped smoking marijuana. He moved out shortly afterwards.

Meanwhile, other strange incidents continued to occur. One of the strangest involved the freezer. They owned a refrigerator with a frost-free freezer.

"One time our freezer would not open," says Carol. "It was stuck for about four days, like it was locked, and when it finally decided to open, there was no frost — no explanation as to why it wouldn't open for days."

The freezer was fine afterwards, and they never had any problems with it.

Carol reports that they also had a problem with strange odors — particularly perfume. After the kids moved out, she decided to make the green room her office. "I would be sitting there at my computer," says Carol, "and all of a sudden I would just be overwhelmed with perfume — just so strong. I'm real sensitive to perfume, and it was like I had to get up and walk out of the room. You couldn't smell it any place else."

Usually when it happened, Carol was alone in the house. She didn't even own perfume and had no idea where the smell could be originating from other than the ghost. The odor was strong enough to linger for about a half hour.

It wasn't long before it happened again. Strangely, on the next occasion, it was a different odor — a different type of flowery perfume. Again, it was so strong she had to leave the room. Thankfully, it quickly dissipated.

One time a friend of Carol's came over.

"Can I use the computer?" he asked. m

"Sure," Carol said. She showed him where it was, and ed, alone in the green room. Several minutes later, her frie It is and said, "You've got a bottle of perfume leaking in soooo strong."

"No, we don't have any perfume," Carol said knowingly, but not saying.

Her friend went back into the room. "It's gone! I don't smell it at all! It's gone!"

Her friend was amazed, so Carol explained to him about their ghost. Needless to say, her friend was convinced. Carol reports that the perfume incident happened about "a couple of times a month for a year and a half."

"You kind of just don't want to believe what you think is going on," says Carol. "You look for some real logical explanation, like we have toxic air…so it was interesting living there — it was very interesting…of course, these are the things they don't tell you when you rent a place."

The Rosses never were able to find out who the ghost was or exactly why the house was haunted. The only thing they discovered was that many people had lived in the home before them, but usually quickly moved out. They stayed longer than anyone else.

Jim and Carol moved out of their home thirty years to the day after they had moved in. They decided the yard and house was too big for just the two of them, so they moved to a smaller home with a smaller yard — and they have not experienced a single ghostly incident in their new home.

Chapter Sixteen

Cemetery Ghosts

Some areas are more likely than others to be haunted by ghosts. Locations such as hotels, theaters, hospitals, schools, and other structures that are used by large numbers of people often show signs of ghostly activity. Very old buildings, such as missions or churches, are also much more likely than most structures to contain a ghost. Among the top of the list, however, are cemeteries and graveyards. Perhaps more than any other location, cemeteries have a reputation for ghostly manifestations, so it should come as no surprise that there is a long list of known haunted graveyards throughout the country.

Why are graveyards so haunted? One obvious reason could be that many people who die remain emotionally attached to their physical body and desire to remain close to it. Another reason is that these locations are where people go when they want to visit their deceased loved ones and the ghosts, also desiring to communicate, may make an appearance.

The Greater Los Angeles area contains a number of well-known haunted graveyards. The Los Angeles Pet Cemetery is one such location. It is here that several celebrities have buried the remains of their beloved pets...some of which have allegedly made random appearances.

Another allegedly haunted location is the Hollywood Memo rial Park Cemetery. One photographer claims to have visited gravesite of screen icon Marilyn Monroe — and took a photo that shows her image.

Forest Lawn

One Los Angeles County graveyard that has earned a reputation for containing ghosts is the well-known Forest Lawn Cemetery. Just off the 34 Freeway in Glendale, Forest Lawn is one of the larger cemeteries in the Southern California area. It is visited by thousands of people every year, each paying their respects to the dead.

In the following case, two young men decided to visit Forest Lawn, not to give their respects, but because it was something to relieve their boredom. They would soon learn to regret their decision. An innocent outing transformed into a terrifying encounter with a very hostile ghost.

The main witness is Larry X, a truck-driver from Southern California. Larry has a friend named Christine, who described him as the kind of guy that people considered a hard-core tough guy. He was large, muscular, and wouldn't allow himself to be pushed around by anybody. He considered himself to be logical, skeptical, and not easily fooled. He was also, says Christine, a very kind man whom she considered a good friend.

Christine has had many personal encounters with ghosts (see my earlier book *California Ghosts*). Larry, however, was skeptical of such things and they often had heated arguments about the subject. Christine would tell Larry about her own experiences, and Larry would shake his head skeptically, telling her that he didn't believe in ghosts and to stop trying to convince him. Then one evening in 1979 or 1980, Christine went over to Larry's house to have dinner with him and his girlfriend. Larry, she says, was a changed man.

"He comes up to me really angry. He's mad. And he says, 'I am so angry!'" says Christine.

"Why?" she asked.

"Because I saw a ghost!" he glared at her. "And I don't believe [illegible]hosts!"

[illegible]h, really?" Christine said, trying to suppress a smile. She [illegible]ed if her skeptical friend had seen something that changed [illegible] about ghosts.

[illegible]be[illegible]ub it in!" Larry said. "I know that you believe in ghosts [illegible] keep trying to shove this stuff down my throat."

Christine apologized and asked Larry to tell her what happened. Larry then revealed his terrifying encounter with a ghost at Forest Lawn, which Christine now relays here:

"He said he was out with a friend of his at Forest Lawn in the middle of the night, around midnight. They were drinking beer, and they went into the chapel section of Forest Lawn. When they entered the chapel, there was a center aisle and there were chairs on either side. There was nobody around. It was dark.

"He said they walked halfway in, and all of a sudden the cross that was at the end of the chapel started glowing and a figure came off the cross and it chased them out of the chapel."

Larry said that he didn't get a very good look at the figure because they were both so scared, but it appeared to be tall and human-looking. It was very bright, but he didn't get a chance to see its face. It moved directly towards them in a manner that Larry felt was menacing and hostile.

The two men ran as fast as they could out of the chapel and across the graveyard. He told Christine that *it* chased them all the way out of Forest Lawn.

"He'd look over his shoulder and see it still behind him," says Christine, "but then, he was running. He said it chased him outside the chapel, into the graveyard, and then after that, they just ran. They didn't look back."

Larry looked at Christine and told her that he had never experienced terror like that before. "It scared him terribly," says Christine. "He said they were both running in terror from this ghost, and it scared him so much that he just wasn't the same anymore. He said it upset him because he had never been afraid of anything in his entire life, and this experience scared him so much that now he's just terrified to see any kind of ghost."

Larry said it was at the main chapel in Forest Lawn where he saw the ghost. Christine speculates that perhaps the area is protected by a spirit or that perhaps the ghost became upset because the two young men were entering the chapel not to pay their respects to the dead, but because they were curious.

"It scared him terribly. He said they were both running in terror and it scared him so much that he just wasn't the same anymore... Now he's just terrified to see any kind of a ghost."

Whatever the case, Larry reports that he will not be returning to Forest Lawn, especially not at night, or anywhere near the chapel.

Another report of ghosts at Forest Lawn involves a group of soldiers seen out in the graveyards, dressed in full uniform and standing at full attention. As soon as the witnesses look away, the soldiers disappear.

Whether this is true or not, judging from the above reports, Forest Lawn appears to be a very good place to encounter a ghost.

Hillcrest Cemetery

However, Forest Lawn is certainly not the only haunted cemetery in the Greater Los Angeles area. One person who knows this firsthand is Hawthorne resident Tony Tocco. From an early age and into his adulthood, Tony has had numerous encounters with ghosts. His many supernatural experiences has inspired within him a strong fascination with the paranormal.

One evening in the mid-1990s, Tony was watching a television program featuring paranormal investigations. The show was discussing a phenomenon called "Electronic Voice Phenomena" or EVP. This technique involves placing an active audio-recording device in an area that is allegedly haunted. The investigator may ask questions out loud or just leave the recording device alone. Afterwards, as the recording is played back, the sounds of mysterious voices can be heard, allegedly originating from the deceased. The theory is that ghosts, using their ability to manipulate electromagnetic energy (for example, turning lights on and off), are able to somehow impress the sound of their voices onto the audiotape.

EVPs, Tony learned, are typically very brief and low in volume. What intrigued him, however, was that it involved a method that could be used — like a Ouija board — to communicate with a spirit while at the same time produce actual physical evidence establishing the reality of ghosts. It was a way to bring the paranormal into the lab for scientific study.

The lure was too strong, and Tony began planning his own investigation into EVPs. He got a small, battery-powered audio recording device and, together with his cousin, looked for a suitable location to launch an investigation.

Already knowing a little bit about the paranormal, Tony knew that ghosts have been reported in cemeteries and graveyards much more often than in most other locations. There was a fairly large cemetery not far from where he lived called Hillcrest Cemetery, located off Inglewood Boulevard and 182nd Street in Inglewood. Tony and his cousin decided to start their investigation there.

They both agreed that late at night would probably be the best time, so late one evening, they drove to Hillcrest Cemetery and sneaked inside the grounds. They walked around and finally picked a gravesite, and set their recorder on top and turned it on. "We'd go to the graves, and we'd set it for about ten minutes on each one. And then we'd just play it back. On some you would hear a little bit of static, and on a couple, you would kind of hear something, but..."

Tony was not impressed with most of the recordings. Although you sometimes did hear noises, none of them were loud enough or clear enough to be conclusive. Yet, there were a few that did have strange noises on them that almost sounded like voices.

Whatever the case, Tony and his cousin were intrigued and inspired enough to continue their investigations. They began to visit other local cemeteries and graveyards, sneaking in late at night with their flashlights and tape recorders. They also tried their experiments during the day, to see if that would be more successful. After all, Tony reasoned, why should the time of day or night matter to a ghost?

Neither Tony nor his cousin were afraid of seeing a ghost — in their minds they could only be so lucky. Instead, they feared what on-lookers might think of what they were doing. "People were probably looking at us kind of weird because we're walking around with our tape recorders over the graves. I thought they might run us out of there because they thought we we're vandalizing, or doing something weird...We were just recording the dead, just talking to dead people. That's all!" says Tony.

While some people did notice them, nobody ever interfered. After many visits to various cemeteries, they began to accrue a sizeable library of apparent EVPs. Again, the vast majority involved short, unexplained noises that really couldn't be identified. However, there were a few that were not as easily explained. And there was at least one EVP from Hillcrest Cemetery that Tony found totally convincing.

"On one of them, we heard very distinctly, saying, 'I'm scared. I'm scared.' And it was like a whisper. It was really weird. We were like, 'Whoa!'" says Tony.

Eventually, Tony and his cousin halted their investigations. However, to this day, Tony feels he captured the voice of a lost and scared spirit hovering near its gravesite at Hillcrest Cemetery.

"I s
ligh gure again, standing there looking at me. He had
and k hair, black blazing eyes, black eyebrows…this hat
hirt…but it wasn't a suit from our times."

Chapter Seventeen

Ghosts of San Fernando Mission

15151 San Fernando Mission Boulevard
Mission Hills, California 91345
818-361-0186

The San Fernando Mission is one of the many well-known haunted locations in the Los Angeles area. Built in 1797, this mission is more than two hundred years old, so it should come as no surprise that it is famous for its ghosts. It's almost a rule in ghost investigations: the older the building, the more likely it will be haunted. Now surrounded by the densely populated suburb of San Fernando, the mission was one of the first structures built in the area.

Today, the structure still retains its old-time charm. Walking among the property is like stepping back two hundred years into the past, to a time before California was a state, when the area was populated by Native Americans, Spanish settlers, missionaries, miners, outlaw bandits, pioneers and settlers, and other colorful characters. Of course, the San Fernando Mission's reputation for being haunted didn't come until much later.

Currently the structure is said to be haunted by an unidentified ghost. Numerous witnesses have reported seeing an apparition roaming among the premises. The majority of the sightings have occurred along the corridors and archways surrounding the building, with one of the ghosts appearing as an apparition walking under the archway late at night. Other witnesses have reported seeing the apparition of an unidentified gentleman with dark hair, wearing an authentic period gaucho costume.

Evidence that the mission is still haunted comes from a new witness. In the late 1980s, friends Kelly and Daniel (not their real names) decided to visit the mission. They arrived and began to explore the rose gardens, fountains, and statues. On this particular day, the mission was crowded with visitors who were planning their future wedding, which would take place at the mission.

Kelly and Daniel walked around and tried to stay out of the way of the wedding planners who were going in and out of the mission, and just enjoying their surroundings. After several moments, the wedding party went back outside, so Kelly and Daniel decided to go inside. This decision led to one of the more unusual experiences in Kelly's life. She had no idea that the structure was allegedly haunted, so what happened next came as a shocking surprise.

"We walked into the mission, and I'm standing there looking all around, and off to the left by this beautiful window I see this figure," says Kelly, "and I told Daniel, 'I don't think they're done here, there's still somebody looking around.'"

Daniel looked at Kelly perplexed. "What are you talking about?" he asked.

Kelly looked around in confusion. The figure she had seen was gone. Pointing, she told Daniel, "There was somebody over there...I just saw somebody standing over there!"

Daniel was still standing in the doorway, so he peered inside and looked around. Nobody else was in the room. "Kelly, there isn't anybody over there," he told her.

Kelly reports that she didn't get a look at the figure because it was on the other side of the room, but said, "It was a male. It had its back to me like it was looking out the window…so I walked down the aisle to the back, and I looked along the wall, and there wasn't anybody there. I walked down the middle aisle and looked where the pews were. Nothing, not a thing. And I thought, okay, that's strange."

Daniel and Kelly were still talking about the encounter several moments later when the wedding party returned and they decided to exit the building. They both assumed the encounter with the ghost — if that's what it was — was over. They were wrong.

Kelly describes what happened next: "We were standing out in front. I was looking over the roses because they had little walkways that you could walk through, and I saw that figure again, standing there looking at me. It had a black jacket on, black pants. This time it had a black hat on. It didn't have a black hat on in the church area. But when I looked at it...*I looked right at it*...and the male looked Hispanic. He had light skin, black hair, black blazing eyes, black eyebrows. You could really see the eyebrows, but it had this hat on and this white shirt. The clothes were a suit-type, but it wasn't a suit from our times. And the hat wasn't a cowboy hat, more kind of like a gaucho. The rose bushes were there, so I couldn't see the bottom half, but the jacket was kind of a shorter jacket. I couldn't see a cumber bun, but it had one of those really thin bolo-ties."

Kelly realized she was seeing the ghost again. Like the first time, she felt almost as if she was paralyzed, and had somehow slipped through a time warp into the past.

"It was like I was in a tunnel-vision. I didn't hear people talking. And all of a sudden I feel somebody tapping heavily on my shoulder, 'Kelly! Kelly!' And I'm watching this figure, and all of a sudden, it turns and it just fades out. It starts to walk away slowly, smiles at me, fades out, and walks away. And Daniel is standing there, saying, 'Kelly! Kelly!' Where have you been?'"

Kelly replied, "I just saw the ghost again! It was a man in period costume, a black hat, white shirt."

"What did he want?" Daniel asked.

"I don't know," Kelly said, "but he smiled at me. He just smiled at me."

Kelly is not a shy person, and she wanted some answers about the ghost she just saw. She decided to ask some questions. The wedding party was just beginning to leave, so she walked up to a group of them and began talking with them. As she suspected, they were planning a wedding. They explained that they had visited the mission many times in the past and sometimes held their events there.

Kelly congratulated them and then dropped the question. She asked, "Have you ever seen a gentleman here dressed in a black jacket with a white shirt, a black hat, a full period costume...like a ghost?"

To Kelly's surprise, one of the young women stepped forward and said, "Did he have black hair and big black eyebrows?"

"Yes!" Kelly exclaimed. "I saw him inside standing by the window. And then I just saw him out here, standing in the rose garden."

The woman replied, "You know, I've never seen him, but my grandmother has seen him. He has appeared to my grandmother. We didn't believe her at first."

"Is your grandmother here?" Kelly asked.

"No, she's no longer alive," the woman told her, "but this figure used to appear to my grandmother and she never knew why, but it would always smile at her."

Kelly thanked the lady for the information and returned to tell Daniel. They were both delighted and surprised to find confirmation of Kelly's sighting so quickly and easily. They spent a few more minutes exploring the location and then left. Kelly remains convinced that she saw an actual ghost.

Today the San Fernando Mission remains open to the public, and tours of the estate are given on a regular schedule.

Chapter Eighteen

Haunts that Border Los Angeles

Within a few hundred-mile radius of Greater Los Angeles, there are literally hundreds of haunted locations — areas where ghostly activity occurs on a regular basis. Below is a list of some of the more famous and actively haunted locations in Greater Los Angeles. In each case, the exact address and phone number of the location is listed so that you can go and visit it yourself and hopefully have your own encounter with the supernatural.

Bella Maggiore Inn

Location: 67 South California Street, Ventura, California 93001; 805-652-0277

The Haunting: The ghost of Sylvia Michaels, a prostitute, allegedly haunts this hotel. In 1947, Sylvia committed suicide by hanging herself in the hotel closet. Since then, sporadic poltergeist-like activity has been reported. In 1994, ghost researcher Richard Senate held a séance. While they apparently made contact with the ghost, the haunting continues. According to the front desk clerk, several recent guests have smelled a rose-scented perfume while others claim to have sensed an invisible presence.

The Comedy Store

Location: 8433 West Sunset Boulevard, Los Angeles, California; 323-650-6268

The Haunting: While this location is now used for entertainment, previously it was called "Ciro's" — a known hangout for gangsters and mobsters. Murders and other violent acts on the property have apparently left it haunted. According to the staff, working comics, and visitors, a wide variety of ghostly activity has occurred here including objects that move by themselves, strange cold spots, weird crashing noises, and phantom voices.

The Conejo Players

Location: 351 South Moorpark Road, Thousand Oaks, California; 805-495-3715

The Haunting: This small community theater is allegedly haunted by a ghost named Alfred who apparently remains a theater critic even after his death. Several actors have reported hearing Alfred stop loudly down the aisle during performances. He has also been blamed for moving props and causing various objects to disappear and reappear in different locations.

Four Oaks Restaurant

Location: 2181 North Beverly Glenn Boulevard, Los Angeles, California; 310-470-2265

The Haunting: This structure was built in 1880 as a stopping point between Los Angeles and the San Fernando Valley. It has served as a hotel, a restaurant, a bar, and a brothel. Today it is allegedly haunted by one ghost — a brightly glowing apparition — whose identity remains unknown.

Hollywood Boulevard and Sierra Bonita (Hollywood, California)

The Haunting: Formerly the location of Native American settlements, numerous witnesses have reported seeing the ghostly apparitions of Indians riding horses, running on foot, shooting arrows and throwing tomahawks. Others have heard loud Indian drumming music. One motorist says he was driven off the road by an apparition of a pioneer covered wagon. Reportedly, it was at this location that hostile Native Americans would attack passing stagecoaches.

Hollywood Entertainment Museum

Location: 7021 Hollywood Boulevard, Los Angeles, California; 323-465-7900

The Haunting: Originally called the Warner Pacific Theater, this building is allegedly haunted by the spirit of the man who helped to build it: Sam Warner. Numerous people have seen his full-color apparition pacing the lobby or sitting in his former office while others have heard strange noises of furniture being moved. Finally, the ghost seems to enjoy causing mischief with the elevator.

Hollywood Memorial Park Cemetery

Location: 6000 Santa Monica Boulevard, Hollywood, California

The Haunting: This cemetery is holds the remains of dozens of well-known Hollywood stars. The ghost of actor Clifton Webb is said to haunt the Abbey of the Psalms Mausoleum. Also, the apparition of an unknown woman dressed in black has often been seen kneeling in front of crypt number 1205.

Laurel Canyon Boulevard and Lookout Mountain (West Hollywood)

The Haunting: A ghostly carriage being pulled by white horses reportedly haunts this particular intersection, located about a half mile on the south side of the mountain pass. In each case, the apparition appears precisely at midnight. Reportedly, the apparition has appeared so suddenly that it has caused car accidents to occur.

Leonis Adobe

Location: 23537 Calabasas Road, Calabasas, California; 818-222-6511

The Haunting: The original owners, Miguel and Espiritu Leonis, are said to be haunting this structure. While still living, the couple jealously guarded their property — and it appears they continue to do so after death. Both employees and visitors have reported ghostly activity, and a book — *Spirits of Leonis* by Rob Wlodarksi — has been written about the case.

Los Angeles Pet Cemetery

Location: 5068 Old Scandia Lane, Calabasas, California

The Haunting: This cemetery holds the remains of the pets of several famous Hollywood stars. For example, Rudolph Valentino's pet Great Dane, "Kabar," was buried here, and since then, witnesses have reportedly heard ghostly panting noises or felt phantom dog-licks near his gravesite. The remains of other famous animals are also buried here including Hop-Along Cassidy's horse and Mary Pickford's dog.

Mann's Chinese Theatre

Location: 6925 Hollywood Boulevard, Hollywood, California; 323-464-8111

The Haunting: The sidewalk outside this theater is reportedly haunted by the ghost of actor Victor Killian, who in 1982, was bludgeoned to death by a man he had met at a nearby bar. The killer was never found. Also, backstage in the theater itself, an unidentified ghost allegedly pulls at the stage curtains and haunts various dressing rooms.

Mission San Buenaventura

Location: 211 East Main Street, Ventura, California; 805-643-4318

The Haunting: Built way back in 1782, this mission is haunted by a ghostly monk with gray hair and a gray robe. The apparition has been seen at many different locations on the estate and beyond, including inside the original adobe structure, in the garden, sitting along the banks of the Ventura River, and even walking along Main Street in Ventura.

The Palace Theater

Location: 1735 Vine Street, Los Angeles, California; 323-467-4571

The Haunting: This location was originally used for stage plays and radio shows, but was later used for television. The ghostly activity here is intense and ongoing and includes an apparition of a man in a Tuxedo, a ghostly older couple, phantom piano playing, lights turning on and off, and objects moving by themselves.

Pantages Theater

Location: 6233 Hollywood Boulevard, Los Angeles, California; 323-468-1770

The Haunting: Pantages Theater was originally used for stage plays, but is today a movie theater. The location has experienced considerable ghostly activity, some of which has been documented by researchers. One investigator successfully recorded the sound of a ghostly singing woman. Most of the activity, however, is attributed to the theater's former owner, Howard Hughes, who purchased the structure in 1949. Another reported ghost is the theater's founder, Alexander Pantages. Most of the activity has manifested as unexplained cold spots and occasional apparitions.

Queen Mary

Location: 1126 Queens Highway, Long Beach, California; 562-435-3511

The Haunting: This location is perhaps the most famous and the most haunted location in Greater Los Angeles. The ghostly activity has been reported by staff workers, visitors, and ghost researchers, and includes the entire range of activity. Some of the haunted locations include the boiler room, the poolroom, and a stateroom. Investigators report that there have been more than six hundred encounters recorded.

Shadow Ranch Park

Location: 22633 Vanowen Street, Canoga Park, California; 818-883-3637

The Haunting: Formerly a ranch estate, this area is now a small public park. A two-story brick and wood ranch house in the center of the park is allegedly haunted by the original owner, Albert Workman, whose apparition has been seen there on numerous occasions. Other reports say that members of the Paul family, who all reportedly died within one week of each other back in the 1930s, haunt the structure.

The Stagecoach Inn Museum

Location: 51 South Ventu Park Road, Newbury Park, California; 805-498-9441

The Haunting: A former hotel, this structure is now a museum. According to the staff, all kinds of strange things happen here, including the appearance of an apparition of a tall, high-society lady who leaves behind a perfumed scent and poltergeist-like activity. The ghosts of an unidentified man and a young boy have also been seen. Famed English psychic medium Sybil Leek once visited the hotel and, during a séance, allegedly made contact with one of the ghosts.

Sweet Lady Jane's Bakery and Restaurant

Location: 8360 Melrose Avenue, Los Angeles, California; 323-653-7145

The Haunting: One of the most famous ghosts that is still allegedly haunting Greater Los Angeles is none other than Orson Welles. One of his favorite places to sit down, relax, and have a bite to eat was Sweet Lady Jane's Bakery and Restaurant. Following his death, Welles apparently still frequents the establishment, as multiple witnesses have seen his ghost sitting at his favorite table. Others have smelled his signature cigar smoke and fine brandy.

Topanga State Park

Location: Entrada Road off Highway 27, Topanga Canyon Boulevard in Topanga Canyon

The Haunting: This location is the source of numerous reports of hauntings. Several homes in the area, which were allegedly built on Native American Burial Grounds, are now experiencing a wide variety of activity that include ghostly footsteps, strange noises, objects moving by themselves, ghostly presences, and unexplained cold spots. Within the park itself, numerous witnesses have reported seeing apparitions of local Chumash and Gabrielano Indians [illegible]sed in full costume. In some of the cases, the Native American [illegible] appear to be angry at the intrusion of people.

Ventura Theater

Location: 26 South Chestnut Street, Ventura, California

The Haunting: This theater is allegedly haunted by the ghost of a young lady who was tragically killed on the location by falling stage lights. Since her death, witnesses have reportedly seen her ghost reliving the accident, her death scream echoing each time. Her glowing apparition has also been seen dancing on the center of the stage where she died.

Westlake On-ramp to Highway 101 (Westlake Village)

The Haunting: Four independent witnesses have reported seeing the apparition of an old man screaming, "Christ is coming!" One man picked up the man, who moments later, disappeared in front of his eyes. Each of the witnesses reported their sighting to the California Highway Patrol.

Westwood Cemetery

Location: 1218 Glendon Avenue, Westwood, California

The Haunting: According to one source, Marilyn Monroe's gho has been seen and photographed near her tomb, located Westwood Cemetery.

William Hart Park and Museum

Location: 24151 San Fernando Road, Newhall, California

The Haunting: William Hart was a famous cowboy actor. Following his death, Hart's estate was converted into a museum. Today, Hart's apparition has been seen wandering the premises. Other witnesses have also reported seeing the apparition of Hart's wife.

Zander Building

Location: 427 East Main Street, Ventura, California

The Haunting: This large public structure today houses several commercial businesses and at least one ghost. The apparition of a tall man wearing a gray suit has been seen in various stores including Eddie's Treasures and The Cat's Meow. Other witnesses have reported seeing the apparition on the rear stairwell to the parking lot. The identity of the ghost remains unknown.

Afterword

The above accounts should only be considered a minor cross-section of the true number of actual hauntings taking place throughout the Greater Los Angeles area. However, they do represent a large enough sampling of the many kinds of hauntings to be able to draw some accurate conclusions about the nature and origin of ghostly phenomena. The above accounts have a great deal to say about what hauntings are, how they start, how they progress, and how they end.

As we have seen, ghosts have played — and continue to play — a powerful and influential role in many people's lives. Although the above accounts are exclusively from the Greater Los Angeles area, they are still surprisingly diverse. We have examined haunted hotels, theaters, hospitals, bookshops, amusement parks, cemeteries, missions, homes, and more.

Clearly, there is no location that is protected from becoming haunted. Wherever there are people, there are ghosts. More than likely, there are hundreds of public hauntings and thousands of private hauntings currently taking place in Southern California.

While we have seen that certain locations such as hotels, theaters, hospitals, and graveyards are more likely than others to have a ghost, the reasons for this seems to correspond to the level o human activity.

In many of the above cases, the origins of the haunting ca linked to the tragic death of one or more persons. ig

In the case of Universal Studios, the sudden death of In girl on one of the amusement rides was the cause of ha nur- the case of the Mount Washington in Glendale invol dden der of a large group of Native Americans. This patt up in death followed by the occurrence of ghostly acti e. numerous other hauntings as well, both public

However, death is not always the cause of some activity. A haunted location can remain inactive until suddenly sparked by a change in the environment. For example, the haunting of the bookshop "The Psychedelic Moon" began when the owners of the shop acquired a set of occult books. Only after the books were disposed of did the haunting activity cease.

Another possible cause for ghosts may not be sudden death, but rather the sheer level of human activity taking place in an area. The case of the Moorpark Melodrama or the Hollywood Roosevelt Hotel is a good example. While these areas are being haunted by spirits, the people who are haunting this area did not necessarily die at that location. The fact that these buildings are very old structures may be an important factor to consider. Interestingly, these cases seem to involve what would be called a "residual haunting" — a sort of echo of past events — as opposed to a ghostly haunting involving actual spirits who are interacting with the physical environment.

Yet another pattern that has exerted itself with the above cases in regards to how hauntings originate is popularly known as the poltergeist. At least three of the witnesses (Brenda Sloan, Tony Tocco, and Claudia Blacios) each reported poltergeist activity occurring during their teenage years. Interestingly, while the poltergeist activity is usually limited to a certain period during early development, each of these witnesses reported having many other encounters later on in life. One possible conclusion is that mediumistic ability may be the trigger that attracts a ghost to a particular person. Some researchers have concluded that poltergeist is a form of uncontrolled mediumship. Whatever the case, it is clear that in some instances, it is a living person who is at least artly responsible for attracting ghost activity.

This is certainly true in cases involving the Ouija Board. At least ree of the cases in this book involve ghostly activity that occurred he direct result of using a Ouija board. In these cases, there was aunting taking place at the time; rather the spirits were called nto a manifestation that resulted in haunting activity.

e have seen, ghostly hauntings can originate in a number nt ways. However, in each case a specific set of circumsually present. In other words, hauntings are not ran- The above cases match what other researchers have discovered — the origin of ghosts is not unexplained. The evidence shows that the origin of ghosts is...people who have died! While this may seem obvious, skeptics have put forth other theories to explain away ghosts as everything from dreams and hallucinations, to misperceptions and outright lies. Instead, however, the cases indicate that ghosts are exactly what they appear to be: the spirits of people who have died.

In fact, ghosts represent some of the best evidence we have of life after death. In many of the above cases — the Hollywood Roosevelt Hotel, Universal Studios, Augustine — the actual identity of the ghost was known. While it is possible that some haunting activity is caused by other unknown agencies, the vast majority of the above cases seem to be attributable to spirits of the deceased.

One of the most fascinating aspects of ghosts is the incredibly wide variety of ways in which they can manifest. Some of the many ghostly manifestations reported in the above cases include apparitions, ghostly footsteps, lights and televisions turning on and off, objects moving by themselves, unexplained odors, animal reactions, bite marks or physical assault, EVPs, and temperature variations.

Cases that are widely separated both geographically and chronologically still follow very similar patterns. In fact, the similarity between the cases is so strong that it not only shows the mechanics of ghostly activity, it argues strongly for the veracity of ghosts. How else could so many people who don't know each other describe ghostly manifestations in nearly identical terms? One good example of this is cases that involve toilets that flush by themselves. Another perhaps better example is the few cases presented that involve doors that cannot be opened, even though they are not locked. This includes not only normal doors, but in one case a freezer door that could not be opened for four day[s]. How ghosts are able to do something like this, however, remains a mystery. Such is the nature of ghosts; there are many questio[ns] that remain about them.

Ghost researchers have discovered that many people a[re able] to see ghosts with their peripheral vision, but not when [looking] directly at them. Several of the cases in this book involved [th]is phenomenon. One possible explanation that has be[en put forth is] that the cones in our eyeballs that capture photon[s] them onto the retina are specialized to capture movement and may be more sensitive to ghostly phenomena than the cones in the center of our retinas.

Whatever the case, ghost researchers have not been able to explain exactly how ghosts manifest as apparitions. Some of the cases involve apparitions that appear transparent. Other apparitions, however, appear to be completely solid. Why this happens continues to remain a mystery.

One curious aspect of ghostly apparitions is the large number of cases in which ghosts can be seen only in the reflection of a mirror. Paranormal researchers long ago discovered that there is a long tradition of paranormal events associated with mirrors. There are many cases in literature telling of this strange association.

Probably the most famous case in this book is the mirror in the Roosevelt Hotel that allegedly reflects the image of Marilyn Monroe. Two other cases also involve apparitions that were seen in mirrors. One case (The Haunted Bookshop) also involves a mirror that seemed to be a source of paranormal activity — it shattered under bizarre circumstances. The question is what is it about mirrors that allow apparitions to become visible? Researchers have offered few explanations. Perhaps it might be related to a similar phenomenon during which people take photographs of spirits that were not visible at the time the photograph was taken, or why spirits are plainly visible to some people and not to others.

The fact that the answer to this and other questions about ghosts has eluded researchers shows that there is still much to learn about the phenomena. Thankfully researchers have been able to provide answers to some of the other mysteries surrounding ghostly phenomena.

Another fascinating feature to hauntings is how long they survive, how they evolve, and how they end. The vast majority of the cases in this book started long ago — and they are still occurring. It s not at all unusual for a haunting to continue for decades on end. f course, the paranormal activity is not occurring one hundred cent of the time. Rather it seems to occur only sporadically.

nterestingly, some of the haunting activity is sparked by certain ions. For example, in the Haunted Hospital case, whenever ould admit a patient into a certain room and hook up a te- ox, the ghost of another nurse would appear and remove the box. In the case of a Haunted Bookshop, it was the presence of occult books on black witchcraft that caused the haunting. The Native American child ghosts of Mount Washington in Glendale seemed to only appear to other local children in the area. In the case of the Haunted Laundry Room, the ghostly activity only occurred if the laundry machine lid was closed. Another ghost, "Clara," appeared to make sure that her living loved ones retrieved a letter that willed them badly needed money.

Interestingly, only a few of the haunting cases were resolved and the activity stopped. One case is the Haunted Laundry Room. In this case the witness spoke out loud to the ghost and was able to reason with it. Although the activity has stopped, it doesn't mean that the ghost isn't still there. In the case of the Haunted Bookshop, the activity dropped sharply after the black magic books were removed from the premises.

For the most part, however, it seems that hauntings are unpredictable and uncontrollable. The obvious exceptions are, of course, the cases involving the Ouija board. In these cases, people initiate encounters with ghosts, and are, in effect, participating in a controlled haunting. As we have seen, however, often the result is that the haunting becomes uncontrolled — and when the weird activity suddenly escalated, the witnesses were able to end the haunting by ceasing to use the Ouija board.

While some of the people in this book who have encountered ghosts were badly frightened by their experiences, an equal number of them found their own experiences interesting or even comforting. However, not all cases were like this. Anybody who says that ghosts cannot hurt you is wrong. In some cases, the ghosts did cause harm to people, including pushing people off of chairs, bite marks and bruises, and even attempted possession. Neverthele most of the witnesses did not feel like they were in any dang

I think the accounts in this book provide strong evide es ghosts are real and that there truly is life after death nily in which witnesses have seen the apparitions of de vid- members provide particularly compelling testim pear- ing corroboration are the cases in which the id endent ance of a ghost is known and reported by m witnesses.

Thankfully today interest in ghosts and "the other side" is growing. More attention and money is being paid towards the research of ghosts and paranormal phenomena. Now real technology is being used to study the presence of ghosts. The use of electromagnetic detectors, infrared photography, motion sensors, audio recorders, ultra-sensitive thermometers, high-definition photography, and more are all being used to successfully capture evidence of ghosts. Interestingly, the more that science and technology has been used to solve the mystery of ghosts, the more the evidence shows that ghosts are real. Researchers and paranormal groups across the United States have now gathered large libraries of photographs, EVPs, EMF readings, and recorded testimonies that all point towards the reality of ghosts.

If you would like to see your own ghost, this is also not that hard to do. There are dozens of locations in Greater Los Angeles that provide excellent opportunities. Again, in most of the cases, the hauntings have been occurring for decades and show no signs of ending. If there is one thing ghost researchers can agree upon, it is that wherever you find people, you will also find ghosts.

Bibliography

Dennett, Preston. *California Ghosts*. Atglen, Pennsylvania: Schiffer Publishing, Ltd. 2004.

Supernatural California. Atglen, Pennsylvania: Schiffer Publishing, Ltd., 2006.

Holzer, Hans. *Hollywood Ghosts*. New York, New York: Bobbs-Merrill Company, Inc., 1974.

May, Antoinette. *Haunted Houses of California*. San Carlos, California: Wide World Publishing/Tetra: 1990, 1993.

Senate, Richard. *Ghost Stalker's Guide to Haunted California*. Ventura, California: Charon, Press, 1998.

Smith, Barbara. *Ghost Stories of California*. Renton, Washington: Lone Pine Publishing, 2000.

Index